I0815130

CAFÉ LAFITTE
IN EXILE

CAFÉ LAFITTE IN EXILE

Queer New Orleans and the Story of America's Oldest Gay Bar

LOUISIANA STATE UNIVERSITY PRESS BATON ROUGE

Published with the assistance of the V. Ray Cardozier Fund

Published by Louisiana State University Press
lsupress.org

Manufactured in the United States of America
First printing

DESIGNER: Barbara Neely Bourgoyne
TYPEFACES: Calluna, text; Lovers in New York and Casablanca URW, display
PRINTER AND BINDER: Sheridan Books, Inc.

JACKET PHOTOGRAPH: *Times Picayune* photo by Sophie Germer.

FRONTISPIECE: View from the balcony of Lafitte House, looking up Bourbon Street toward Canal, ca. 1959. In the foreground is 941 Bourbon Street, the original home of Café Lafitte. The Historic New Orleans Collection, The Franck-Bertacci Collection, acc. no. 1994.94.2.942.

LIBRARY OF CONGRESS CATALOGING-IN-PUBLICATION DATA

Names: Perez, Frank, 1968– author | Palmquist, Jeffrey author
Title: Café Lafitte in Exile : queer New Orleans and the story of America's oldest gay bar / Frank Perez and Jeffrey Palmquist.
Description: Baton Rouge : Louisiana State University Press, [2026] | Includes bibliographical references and index.
Identifiers: LCCN 2025045788 (print) | LCCN 2025045789 (ebook) | ISBN 978-0-8071-8584-1 (cloth) | ISBN 978-0-8071-8664-0 (epub) | ISBN 978-0-8071-8665-7 (pdf)
Subjects: LCSH: Café Lafitte in Exile (New Orleans, La.)—History | Gay bars—Louisiana—New Orleans—History | Gay people—Louisiana—New Orleans—History | Sexual minorities—Louisiana—New Orleans—History
Classification: LCC HQ76.3.U52 N47 2026 (print) | LCC HQ76.3.U52 (ebook)
LC record available at https://lccn.loc.gov/2025045788
LC ebook record available at https://lccn.loc.gov/2025045789

For all the former and current employees of
Café Lafitte in Exile, especially the "woodchips"

CONTENTS

ILLUSTRATIONS

ILLUSTRATIONS

CAFÉ LAFITTE
IN EXILE

Introduction

We wrote *In Exile: The History and Lore Surrounding New Orleans Gay Culture and Its Oldest Gay Bar* between 2009 and 2011. The fifteen years or so between then and now might as well have been a lifetime. Much has changed since the book first appeared, both for us personally and also for the bar itself. We each have different partners now as well as different career paths. Jeffrey is a full-time real estate agent now, and I've been busy with a nonprofit organization I cofounded shortly after *In Exile* was published. Our perspective now is more expansive than it was fifteen years ago.

The bar has changed too. All the Lafitte's bar staff from 2011 are gone, as are many of the old-time regulars. Some have moved away, some have lost interest in the bar, and far too many have died. Among the cadre of colorful characters who have since passed on were Rip and Marsha Naquin-Delain, fixtures not only at the bar but also in the French Quarter for nearly forty years. Their loss coincided with, and in some ways resulted in, larger changes in the French Quarter's gay community.

The Quarter and its queer community, especially the bar scene, was also profoundly affected by the COVID-19 pandemic. Some bars did not survive the citywide shutdown, while others limped along on life support. Today many have yet to fully recover. The most visible change has been that several bars are no longer open twenty-four hours a day.

Yet another change in recent years has been the amount of scholarship on queer New Orleans history. When *In Exile* was published, the only other book related to local LGBT+ history was Johnny Townsend's *Let the Faggots Burn* (2011), which was essentially a compilation of biographical sketches of the victims of the tragic 1973 arson at the Up Stairs Lounge. Since then, several books on various aspects of New Orleans queer history have come out: Clay Delery's *The Up Stairs Lounge Arson* (2014) and *Out for Queer Blood: The Murder of Fernando Rios and the Failure of New Orleans Justice* (2017); our anthology *My Gay New Orleans* (2016); Howard P. Smith's *Unveiling the Muse: The Lost History of Gay Carnival in New Orleans* (2017) and *A Sojourn in Paradise: Jack Robinson in 1950s New Orleans* (2020); Robert Fieseler's *Tinderbox: The Untold Story of the Up Stairs Lounge Fire and the Rise of Gay Liberation* (2018); Howard P. Smith and Frank Perez's *Southern Decadence in New Orleans* (2018); and Frank Perez's *Political Animal: The Life and Times of Stewart Butler* (2022). In 2023, Townsend updated and expanded his earlier work, which was published as *Inferno in the French Quarter: The UpStairs Lounge Fire.* Also, the number of documentary films about queer New Orleans history has grown from just one in 2010 to at least six in 2023. In addition, the popularity of podcasts and a handful of oral history projects have contributed to the growing knowledge of queer New Orleans history.

Much of this growing body of knowledge has been facilitated by the LGBT+ Archives Project of Louisiana—a nonprofit organization dedicated to the preservation of queer history in Louisiana. This statewide collective was founded as a result of the research we have conducted in exploring local queer history. I currently serve as the organization's executive director, and Jeffrey chairs one of its standing committees.

Café Lafitte in Exile: Queer New Orleans and the Story of America's Oldest Gay Bar begins with a meditation on place and identity. This introduction, along with the epilogue, serve as contextual bookends for the detailed historical narrative found between the opening and closing chapters. Chapter 1 addresses queer New Orleans before the advent of gay bars (as we understand that term) and offers a discussion of Indigenous queerness, a topic that received only a passing mention earlier. We examine what scarce written references to queerness European colonizers left behind in order to fully appreciate how deep this area's queer history is. We also discuss nineteenth-century New Orleans figures who were, or may have been, gay, including the writers Baron Ludwig Reizenstein and Walt Whitman. Reizenstein's work is particularly interesting for its insights into the lesbian scene in the 1850s. Also making a debut appearance in this book is the Reverend Carl Schlegel, the New Orleans minister whose queer advocacy in the early 1900s was not rediscovered until a few years ago. Chapter 2 examines the bar in its original location, including biographical information about the original bar owners and a handful of their more notable regular patrons. We also consider the role gay men played in the preservation of the French Quarter in the early twentieth century. This chapter also investigates the mythology that has grown up around the building at 941 Bourbon Street (Lafitte's Blacksmith Shop) and the reason the bar relocated in 1953.

Chapter 3 opens by detailing the bar's relocation to its present site. In it, we recount a tragic gay-bashing murder, in which the bar played a key role. The chapter also closely examines the emergence of the bar's gay identity and why that was important in a very homophobic time. More specifically, we investigate the city of New Orleans's aggressive crackdown on gay bars in the 1950s. We discuss Gay Carnival and the Southern Decadence festival, and we conclude the chapter with the burgeoning gay liberation movement of the 1970s, a time when the bar was sold to its current owner. Chapter 4 explores the early years of Tom Wood's proprietorship of the bar. We discuss the bar's acquisition of the Bourbon Street Awards as well as the addition of the gallery to the exterior of the building. We detail the gradual shifts, and setbacks, in the city's homophobic attitudes, including an attack by the police on the bar's owner in the bar itself. There is also a section on the famed gay artist George Dureau, before we turn our attention to an appraisal of the HIV/AIDS crisis. Chapter 5 opens with Hurricane Katrina and outlines the bar's history from that time to the present day. The chapter also examines how the role of the bar has evolved as widespread acceptance of queerness has grown in recent decades. We draw a contrast between the bar's devoted gay patronage after Katrina to the loss of that patronage today; further, the chapter asks why that loss has occurred and addresses the criticism that the bar should no longer be considered gay. The book concludes by reflecting on the challenges of researching and writing queer history. The last chapter addresses issues such as the lack of primary source material and the challenges associated with archival records. It also acknowledges the problems of oral history, on which part of this book relies. The chapter closes with a meditation on memory and identity.

We have also interviewed Tom Wood, the current owner of Café Lafitte in Exile. We attempted to interview him fifteen years ago, when we were researching our first book, but his general manager at the time, whom we did interview, told us Wood would not agree to it. Later, after the book was published, we learned from a subsequent general manager that Wood was puzzled and annoyed that we hadn't reached out to him.

PLACE AND IDENTITY

It is early Saturday morning. As day gradually usurps night, I sit pensively in Jackson Square. The cobblestone banquettes are shiny with wet, for the street cleaners have just made their rounds washing away the remains of yesterday. Nearby a few homeless people sleep on benches, sitting upright, while a pigeon or two search in vain for crumbs. For the most part, the Square is empty, save a few faithful awaiting early-morning Mass. A family of tourists ambles by with their luggage. In the corner, a fortune teller shuffles her tarot cards. An old man walks his dog. The stench of trash fills the air as a garbage truck shares the streets with several produce delivery trucks bringing what will be, in a few hours, brunch. A strong breeze from the river is blowing.

The Cathedral bells ring, and about two dozen people file into the church for Mass, myself included. No, I am not here to worship, nor am I here to eat *ecce pannis angelorum;* I am here to imagine. You see, for me, St. Louis Cathedral (and the French Quarter in general) is a time machine. As the liturgy drones on, I imagine what it must have been like two hundred years ago, when this church would have been packed for an early-morning Lenten Mass. This ability to awaken a sense of history—to really make the past come alive—is one of the qualities that make the French Quarter so magical.

After the Mass has ended, I sit in the Square chatting with an ancient nun dressed in full pre–Vatican II regalia. She is disappointed to learn I will not be attending Mass regularly but informs me I am welcome anytime. Her wrinkled face offers me a smile and a blessing, and she departs for whatever her day has for her, part of which will no doubt include cyclical recitations of the rosary. As she wanders off down St. Ann Street, I wonder what she will think of the men sitting in the gay bars a few blocks away she will pass momentarily. Perhaps she will give them no thought at all. Nor they her. Not far away, the oldest gay bar in the country peacefully coexists a few blocks from the oldest Roman Catholic convent in the country. That's about as New Orleans as it gets.

Many words come to mind when one thinks of "New Orleans," but my favorite is *mélange,* a word that comes to us from the seventeenth-century French word *mêler,* which means "to mix and mingle" and which has its etymological roots in the Old French word *mesler,* a euphemism for sexual intercourse during the Renaissance. Yes, *mélange* is the perfect word to describe New Orleans, for what else is this city but a multicultural orgy producing a linguistic, ethnic, culinary, musical, and architectural fusion—disparate histories and cultural traditions melding, blending, coalescing, uniting, yet each one never quite losing its own identity. Ezra Pound might call it the urban embodiment of vorticism.

These thoughts are heavy, too heavy to bear without coffee, so I walk a block to Café du Monde. Abandoning medieval French etymology, my mind turns to chicory. Chicory is a staple ingredient in virtually all authentic New Orleans coffee. A derivative of the endive plant, chicory has been a coffee additive (and sometimes a substitute) for centuries. The chicory flower is thought to be the inspiration of the *Blaue Blume,* a central symbol in German Romanticism that represents desire and metaphysical yearning for the unattainable and the infinite—two universal concepts at the heart of Romanticism and essential to any brand of hedonism. No wonder New Orleanians love chicory!

The chicory's stimulating quality casts a spell on me, and I consider the *Blaue Blume* in terms of the mystery of sexual identity. What makes the intersection of sexuality and the urban space we call New Orleans so unique, so electric, so free?

Something about New Orleans renders difference irrelevant, makes it melt. *Melt* is a good word to describe the French Quarter. Everything seems to melt here: cares, worries, inhibitions. Especially inhibitions. But not just morality, other things melt too: cultures, ethnicities, architecture, cuisine, music, languages. And sexualities. It's not so much evanescence but rather mutability, a melting into each other, like the outlying marsh and swamp, where land melts into sea. History melts too, if we let it.

Four hours after his first arrival in New Orleans, Tennessee Williams wrote in his journal, "Here, surely, is the place I was made for."[1] It is likely that his first sexual experience with a man occurred a few nights later. Williams would later call New Orleans his "spiritual home" and the French Quarter "the last frontier of Bohemia." As he once wrote to a friend, "Town is wide open."[2]

Wide open indeed. Never burdened by the Puritanical baggage that straddles so many other American cities, New Orleans has always enjoyed a certain permissiveness. Hedonism permeates the air, so to speak. The city's history and reputation for letting the good times roll is well documented: Storyville and its sex workers, jazz-filled bordellos, opium dens, the supposed birth of the cocktail, a love of gambling, Carnival, the nonstop drinking. But a significant part of New Orleans's debauched past remains curiously hidden.

Despite the progress made in recent years, much of American queer history remains in the closet. This is certainly true of New Orleans. And that's a shame. After all, New Orleans, throughout its colorful and picaresque history, has inspired and offered refuge to multitudes of gay writers, artists, musicians, and philanthropists. At some point during their time in New Orleans, each one of them, along with thousands of anonymous others, undoubtedly darkened the door of America's oldest gay bar—Café Lafitte in Exile.

Ancient mythology is perhaps the greatest triumph of humankind's ability to imagine, and the Muses in particular are the personification of our greatest artistic and intellectual aspirations. Born of a coupling between Zeus and Mnemosyne (memory), their lineage suggests a timeless truth: that history and imagination are inextricably linked together. New Orleans, a city that embraces and respects its history, cannot help then but be a wellspring of creativity. Imagination provides meaning and understanding to knowledge; it helps us perceive and thus shape our various realities.

Much of gay history is lost, and that is certainly regrettable. In the course of researching this book, we have asked gay New Orleanians—young and old—to remember. Their recollections form much of the narrative that follows. But memory is not perfect, and throughout the book we have identified several myths that constitute the lore surrounding Café Lafitte in Exile. New Orleanians are fond of saying, "Never the let the truth get in the way of a good story." Here we have attempted to set the facts straight without sacrificing some of those stories.

As much as this book is about the history of queer New Orleans, it is also a book about New Orleans itself. It is part reporting, part revealing, part investigating, part questioning. It is partly scholarly, partly gossipy. It is wholly a love letter, not only to the city but also to the queer men and women who contribute greatly to its complexity and beauty. Thoroughly exhaustive, comprehensive histories of other aspects of queer New Orleans history remain to be written; this book is but a step in the direction of a larger picture. Here we have focused on the city's oldest gay bar, positioning that discussion in the larger context of queer New Orleans history. In the process, we have created a general timeline of the major events, people, and attitudes that have shaped the queer community in New Orleans throughout its history.

—FRANK PEREZ

1

BULBANCHA WAS QUEER

Long before René-Robert Cavelier, sieur de La Salle claimed Louisiana for France and before Jean-Baptiste Le Moyne de Bienville founded New Orleans, there was something queer about the trading post on the sharp bend in the Mississippi River where the French Market now exists. Before Bienville, who lived into his eighties and never married, dubbed the area "La Nouvelle Orleans," the Natives called it "Bulbancha"—a Choctaw/Chickasaw word meaning "place of many tongues."[1]

The confluence of waterways that characterize southern Louisiana in general and the Mississippi Delta in particular serves as a metaphor for the amalgamation of cultural influences that made this area distinctive long before the Europeans arrived. Bulbancha was not only a place of many languages; it was also a place of many sexualities.

Sixteenth-century French and Spanish colonizers were shocked to discover gender-bending Indigenous people as they sailed down the Mississippi River. Sometimes broadly referred to as "Two Spirits," queer Natives were ubiquitous. Even more shocking to the European colonizers was the fact that two-spirited people were highly regarded by their tribes. In 1751, French Navy captain Jean Bernard Bossu wrote of the Choctaw, "They are morally quite perverted, and most of them are addicted to sodomy."[2] Apparently, the Great

Spirit on this side of the Atlantic was much more gender fluid and tolerant than the Abrahamic deity who arrived on these shores in the fifteenth century.

An exploration of the vast and incredibly diverse nature of Indigenous sexualities is beyond the scope of this work, but it is important to remember that our understanding of Native sexuality and their notions of gender are limited by modern biases and the association of Indigenous people as "a thing of the past." This perception stems in part from the ways our thinking has become so colonized. In their study of Indigenous queerness, Manuela Picq and Josi Tikuna note: "Language shows that Indigenous queerness, in its own contextual realities, predates the global LGBT framework. Yet Indigenous experiences are rarely perceived as a locus of sexual diversity. This is partly because Indigenous people are imagined as remnants of the past, whereas sexual diversity is associated with political modernity."[3] The colonization and erasure of Indigenous people include not only their land, language, and culture but also their sexualities. New Orleans–based Ishak scholar Jeffrey Darensbourg has rightly pointed out that Indigenous nations recognized and respected the existence of more than two genders and conducted marriages between people of the same gender. The legacy of acceptance of LGBT+ people has a deep history locally.

What little we know of Indigenous notions of sexuality and gender roles stems from colonial records (mostly letters and travel writings) and does not paint a comprehensive picture but does establish that Indigenous people did not subscribe to a strictly male-female binary. And despite their biases and colonial point of view, these primary sources also firmly establish that the role and status of women was very different in Indigenous cultures than what the colonizers were accustomed to. This challenged colonial heteronormativity. For example, when Sauvole, the first colonial governor of Louisiana, made initial contact with the Bayougoula people, their leader, a man named Antobiscania, was incensed because Sauvole treated his wife rudely. Antobiscania then chastised Sauvole and lectured him on how women should be treated with respect. Sauvole later wrote that he "had not considered the savages were sensitive in that manner."[4] An early lieutenant in the French military, Jean-François-Benjamin Dumont de Montigny, wrote of the Houma, "It is a masculine woman who appears to be the most esteemed."[5] And a Jesuit priest, Pierre-François Xavier de Charlevoix, recorded of the Natchez, "There is among that

Bulbancha Is Still a Place zine cover, 2019. The area we now call New Orleans was first called "Bulbancha" by Indigenous people.

nation a woman chief who has as much authority as the Grand Chief."[6] The Natchez were one of the larger Indigenous groups in Louisiana and serve as a case study in how Native gender roles differed from European ones.

Scholars have described the first few centuries after initial European contact with Indigenous people as a "shatter zone," meaning the various Indigenous groups of the southeastern United States experienced great upheavals and profound changes resulting from epidemics for which they had no immunity and the slave trade sponsored by the British colonies' alliance with the Chickasaw.[7] For the most part, Indigenous groups responded to the Shatter Zone by resisting or fleeing—communal fight or flight. But in the Lower Mississippi Valley, the Natchez were different.

Like the Borg in *Star Trek,* the Natchez strategy was to absorb outsiders—and women played a key role in that absorption. Outsiders such as traders, missionaries, and even men from other tribes were married to Natchez women and expected to follow the leader of the Natchez nation—the Great Sun. Women played a key role in Natchez society. That society was highly stratified, and those at the top were known as "Suns." (The Natchez called themselves "People of the Sun.") Female Suns helped form policy toward Europeans, served as diplomats when negotiating with Europeans, and facilitated a relatively peaceful relationship with the French.[8] This would change, however, in the 1720s.

Because of their adaptability to the shifting tides of the shatter zone, the Natchez survived far longer than many of their counterparts, most of whom had died off or faded away. Many groups who had been decimated and displaced were assimilated into Natchez villages and culture.[9] By the time Louisiana was being colonized by the French in the late seventeenth and early eighteenth centuries, the Natchez nation was the last of the great Mississippian chiefdoms.

Other colonial records strongly suggest the existence, and acceptance, of cross-dressing. Describing some Natchez men in the 1720s, Montigny writes, "They wear their hair long and in braids, and wear skirts like the women."[10] Another French priest, François Le Maire, also expresses moral concern when describing some of the Natchez, "men who dress like women and are excluded from all the work of men."[11] There are also written accounts of a great female Tunica leader who dressed as a man during her life and who was buried in upper-class French menswear. Although the colonizers had no word to describe it at the time, it's safe to assume some of these people were what today would be considered transgender. They may have also been representations of what some anthropologists have described as multiple genders.

Indigenous queerness was so common that Bienville himself commented on the subject. When a French military officer named Ladun complained to the colonial governor about it, Bienville's response was recorded in a 1720 entry in Ladun's journal: "There were young men who seemed to have renounced their sex in order to serve uses so contrary to nature; that they were no longer received in the society of men, and that they carried like a woman a band of skin which covered them in front, from the waist to the knees. He also warned that they were pushing youth so far, that at the age of fifty they did not return to their natural state, and that the savages still used them."[12]

One of the earliest written references to homosexuality in colonized New Orleans dates to 1724, just six years after the city was founded and appears in the record of a criminal trial. When the *Bellone* docked at the port, it was soon discovered that its captain, a man named Beauchamp, was in a sexual relationship with his teenaged cabin boy. He was called before the French Superior Council, the governing authority at the time, which essentially "slapped him on the wrist" by assigning the cabin boy to a different ship, thus sparing the captain a harsher punishment, such as prison. But Captain Beauchamp would not be denied the object of his affection. After the boy was reassigned to another ship, the captain snuck aboard at night and took the boy back, returned to the *Bellone,* and sailed down the river under cover of darkness. In the morning, the French Superior Council gave chase but to no avail. The saga of Captain Beauchamp and his cabin boy ended sadly, when the *Bellone* later sank off the coast of Alabama.[13]

The first Louisiana Criminal Code (1805) prescribed a mandatory life sentence for indulging in "the abominable and detestable crime against nature." Later the penalty was reduced to ten years in prison, and later still, to five years. According to journalist Robert Fieseler: "Subsequent revisions to the penal code in the twentieth century reduced the mandatory penalty—by 1942 the minimum sentence was two years in prison with hard labor optional—but the stigma surrounding same-sex acts rendered non-heterosexuals a criminal class. Heterosexual citizens who attacked or robbed sex 'deviates' (a common midcentury term used by police and public officials to describe homosexuals) were rarely charged or convicted, as such victims were considered to be outside the law's protection."[14] The state's anti-sodomy law wasn't struck down until 2003, when the United States Supreme Court handed down *Lawrence v. Texas.*[15]

Despite these social and legal obstacles, queer people lived in New Orleans from its inception unable to openly express their true natures yet making incredible contributions to the city's cultural complexity nonetheless. Little is known of the doubtless thousands of LGBT+ people who lived in and passed through New Orleans for the balance of the eighteenth and much of the nineteenth centuries. Being queer was obviously not something people wanted to document (to do so could result in arrest, the loss of a job, institutionalization, familial and societal ostracization, eviction, and in some cases, suicide); therefore, primary source material is scarce.

THE NINETEENTH CENTURY

Despite the rarity of such material, researchers today are aware of a handful of gay and lesbian people (and have suspicions about others) in nineteenth-century New Orleans. Some contemporary scholars theorize prominent businessman and early New Orleans philanthropist John McDonogh (1779–1850) was probably gay. A lifelong bachelor who was described as eccentric and reclusive, McDonogh amassed a fortune in real estate and the shipping business, the bulk of which (roughly two million dollars) he willed to New Orleans and his native Baltimore upon his death for the purpose of establishing schools for poor white and free Black children.[16] Many schools in New Orleans today still bear his name. McDonogh also donated the original tract of land that became New Orleans City Park. McDonough has become controversial in recent years for having been an enslaver. We do not know if McDonough was gay, but if he was, his legacy of public education is just one of many unattributed contributions LGBT+ people have made to the city.

In 1848, two years before McDonogh died, Walt Whitman (1819–92) arrived in the city. He was twenty-nine years old. He only stayed a few months, but his short time in New Orleans had a long impact. English professor T. R. Johnson writes: "Something happened to Walt Whitman during his short stay in New Orleans . . . A breakthrough, an awakening, an epiphany, whatever it was, it laid the groundwork for the most innovative and influential body of work in all of U.S. literature."[17] Precisely what Whitman's eureka moment was in the spring of 1848 is impossible to determine. At the time, New Orleans was one of the largest cities and busiest ports in the nation. Surely the city's racial diversity (much more diverse than his native Brooklyn at the time) fascinated him. And the sensory imagery for which New Orleans is so well known must have overwhelmed him. But was there something else? Something more? It is probable Whitman had his first sexual encounter with another man while visiting New Orleans. This is speculation, of course, but what is certain is that the city greatly influenced Whitman's later poetry. Literary scholar Ed Folsom argues Whitman found his first-person poetic voice in New Orleans, and poet

Walt Whitman at about the time he was in New Orleans, 1854.
Samuel Hollyer's steel engraving of Whitman served as the frontispiece
to the first edition of *Leaves of Grass,* published on July 4, 1855.
Library of Congress Prints and Photographs Division.

Nordette Adams writes, "The Crescent City directly influenced Whitman's beliefs about human rights and the power of the individual voice."[18]

Scholar Robert K. Martin has noted that Whitman's New Orleans experience "had an important impact on his conception of male love" as reflected in his homoerotic poems.[19] In "Once I Pass'd Through a Populous City," a poem about New Orleans, he wrote, "I remember only a woman I casually met there who detain'd me for love of me."[20] But Martin insightfully observes that this line was changed. Whitman's original line read: "I remember only the man who wandered with me, there, for love of me." In another poem, "I Saw in Louisiana a Live-Oak Growing," he exulted that the "rude, unbending, lusty" tree made him "think of manly love."[21]

> I saw in Louisiana a live-oak growing,
> All alone stood it and the moss hung down from the branches,
> Without any companion it grew there uttering joyous leaves of
> dark green,
> And its look, rude, unbending, lusty, made me think of myself,
> But I wonder'd how it could utter joyous leaves standing alone there
> without its friend near, for I knew I could not,
> And I broke off a twig with a certain number of leaves upon it, and
> twined around it a little moss,
> And brought it away, and I have placed it in sight in my room,
> It is not needed to remind me as of my own dear friends,
> (For I believe lately I think of little else than of them,)
> Yet it remains to me a curious token, it makes me think of manly love;
> For all that, and though the live-oak glistens there in Louisiana
> solitary in a wide flat space,
> Uttering joyous leaves all its life without a friend a lover near,
> I know very well I could not.[22]

This poem was originally conceived as one of a series of "Live Oak with Moss" poems in the Calamus section of the 1860 edition of *Leaves of Grass.* Before selecting the Calamus root as the primary metaphor for gay attachment, Whitman considered using the live oak tree. In the poem, Whitman negotiates the tension between "the desire to withdraw from conventional society into a protected homosexual subculture and the pain of unrequited homoerotic longings."[23]

A deep-seated yearning for male affection and the compelling pressure to suppress that need is a major theme in much of Whitman's early poetry, and it's a theme to which anyone who has ever been in the closet can certainly relate. That a live oak tree could utter joyous leaves in its solitude seems to offer hope, but the poet questions that paradox's sustainability.

Where Whitman found "manly love" in New Orleans, if he did at all, is uncertain. Gay social networking for the purpose of finding sex partners has been around for centuries. Fifteenth-century Florence, for example, had quite an extensive network, a Renaissance version of Grindr, if you will. It's safe to assume nineteenth-century New Orleans also had such a network. Activist and historian Roberts Batson describes nineteenth-century New Orleans this way: "Throughout its history, a vibrant same-sex social world flourished underground in the sensual city. In the late nineteenth century, one of the most colorful brothel owners, Fanny Sweet, was described as 'Thief, lesbian, Confederate spy, poisoner and procurer.'"[24] Sex tourism is an industry as old as the city itself, and throughout the city's history, there have been well-known red-light districts such as the Swamp, Gallatin Street, and Storyville.

A glimpse into the nineteenth-century "gay scene" in New Orleans can be found in the work of Baron Ludwig von Reizenstein (1826–85). Reizenstein was a German expatriate sent to the United States in 1849 for "personal instability and possibly sexual deviance."[25] In 1848, Reizenstein's father wrote: "On returning to Munich from my mission, I found my son Ludwig absent and it was only after several days of searching in town that he was at last discovered in Brunthal, a resort for residents of Munich, where he had quartered himself together with a friend of his persuasion, a young Count Voltolini, and both of them had been living it up at my expense."[26] Reizenstein scholar and translator Steven Rowan notes: "This passage is the only one hinting that Ludwig might have been homosexual, since the phrase *seiner Uberzeugung* here translated as 'of his persuasion' could be interpreted that way. The delicacy with which Baron Alexander danced around the subject was precisely the same way he had handled questions of his wife's sexuality five years before."[27]

Whatever Reizenstein's sexuality was, he had no qualms writing about "the love that dare not speak its name." Upon arriving in New Orleans, he secured a job as a property surveyor and painter of real estate sales posters in order to pay the bills, but his real passion was writing. In his spare time, he wrote a novel, *Die Geheimnisse Von New Orleans* (*The Mysteries of New Orleans*), which was published serially in *Louisiana Staats-Zeitung* during 1854 and 1855. Some have suggested a better translation would be "The Secrets of New Orleans." In the book, there is a chapter titled "Lesbian Love," which features a love affair between two female characters, Claudine and Orleana. The dialogue is erotic.

> Oh how the fresh warmth of your proud neck drives me wild.
> How your breasts make my blood boil!
> Orleana, Orleana how excitedly loose your clothes are!
> Claudine, Claudine how tightly you are corseted!

Reizenstein concludes the chapter by writing:

> New Orleans is the Meran of the United States for lesbian ladies,[28] where they hold their mysterious gatherings, unhindered and unseen by the Argus-eyes of morality until now . . . We find them in clubs of twelve to fifteen . . . all along the entire left side of the New Basin . . . They have lost their earlier location on Lake Pontchartrain. They were driven out in part through the efforts of old McDonough. We could not determine whether they have resumed their previous location now that McDonough has been dead for several years . . . The moon smiled knavishly and the stars glittered with delight as they spotted Cupid flying down Toulouse Street, blushing red from head to foot, with flaccid bow and empty quiver.[29]

The reference to lesbian spaces along the New Basin Canal and Lake Pontchartrain is curious and raises questions. Were these real places? If so, what did these spaces look like? Were they bars? Parks? Private residences? Who were the lesbians that frequented these places? And is the "McDonough" mentioned in the passage the John McDonogh introduced earlier in this chapter? John McDonogh had indeed died prior to the publication of *The Mysteries of*

New Orleans, and he certainly would have the social standing and political connections to expel a colony of lesbians anywhere in the city. And if this passage does refer to John McDonogh, is this a case of him protesting too much?

But lesbians aren't the only departure from heteronormativity in the novel. Rowan observes: "Virtually everyone else in the book displays perverted sexuality: the effeminate cross-dressing dandy Emil, the equally effeminate architect Albert, Emil's amoral hooker-lover Lucy, the drunken sexist 'Cocker' Hahn, the murderous, sadistic priest Dubreuil, the necrophiliac rapist Lajos, the timorously incestuous repressed lesbians Frida and Jenny, and even the native North German cook Urschl (who becomes in all likelihood the only white female in nineteenth-century American fiction to have had her sexual encounter with a black male portrayed as a comic episode)."[30]

Criticism of the novel was predictably swift and fierce. Describing the work as disgusting and lacking propriety and being morally decadent, one reviewer wrote, " Whoever makes wit of such things before unprepared ears and allows his muse to bathe in the vicious waters of *Venus vulgivaga* is immoral."[31] When a rival German newspaper attacked the work as indecent, Reizenstein countered in a column of his own, charging the rival paper was read by "shy, superannuated virgins unwilling to look any man in the eye."[32]

Part of the alarm may have stemmed from the fact the characters were thinly veiled representations of actual New Orleanians. At least one reader speculated that Orleana was the daughter of the fabled Micaela Almonester, Baroness de Pontalba. Other readers assumed other characters were based on other people. Reizenstein responded to this conjecture by stating, "We could not find a place for your other comments about *The Mysteries of New Orleans* because they penetrate too deeply into the affairs of well-known families, and we do not feel entitled to violate our discretion in this direction."[33]

Initially, Reizenstein dismissed his critics and defended his book, arguing that it was an exposé of societal hypocrisy, but later he seems to have regretted writing the book and called it a "sin of youth." He continued to write and even penned another novel. He also achieved some fame as an entomologist in 1863, when he published *Catalogue of the Lepidoptera of New Orleans and Its Vicinity.* Scholar Steven Rowan has concluded that Reizenstein may "be seen as a bizarre Teutonic avatar of Tennessee Williams."[34]

Jazz pianist Tony Jackson, ca. 1907–16. William Russell Jazz Collection at The Historic New Orleans Collection, acquisition made possible by the Clarisse Claiborne Grima Fund, acc. no. 92-48-L.241.

Whatever gay-friendly bars existed in mid-nineteenth-century New Orleans, if any, are lost to history. The earliest gay business establishment in New Orleans that we know of was a brothel run by a burly male madam known as Miss Big Nelly in the late 1800s. This house was located in "Black Storyville," an area adjacent to "white" Storyville across Canal Street. Reportedly, the house was the scene of "large scale, noisy interracial functions."[35] At the turn of the century, there was also the Frenchman's, a small jazz club in Storyville which was popular among cross-dressers.[36]

One of the Frenchman's star attractions was Tony Jackson (1876–1921). Jackson was highly influential in the early development of jazz and was widely considered the unrivaled king of jazz pianists. He mentored the likes of Jelly Roll Morton and others. Jackson's hit song "Pretty Baby" was written about another man, possibly his lover, a fact that informs the song's suggestive double entendres. Composed in the Frenchman's saloon in the early years of the twentieth century, it was not published until 1916, and then with new, sanitized lyrics tailored for Fanny Brice to perform in the Broadway musical *Passing Show.* Jackson lived openly as a gay Black man in New Orleans but eventually moved to Chicago in 1912 in search of greater freedom. He is credited with helping Chicago become a center of jazz. In addition to his musical talent, Jackson was unrivaled as a showman. According to the Chicago LGBT Hall of Fame, into which he was inducted in 2011: "He is remembered for dancing an impressive high-kicking cakewalk while playing . . . Even his personal sartorial style came to define the archetypical image of the ragtime pianist: gray derby, ascot with diamond stickpin, a checkered vest, and sleeve garters."[37] After his death at age forty-four, he was remembered as "an epileptic, alcoholic, homosexual Negro genius."[38]

But while Jackson could be openly gay in Storyville and Miss Big Nelly could run a brothel nearby for gay men, queerness in Storyville was limited to lesbianism. "The District," as it was officially called, featured "sporting houses" that offered lesbian sex shows and ménage à trois experiences. The Sapho House provided such experiences exclusively. Other venues incorporated lesbianism into their bill of fare; for example, Madam Emma Johnson's sex circus included a "Dyke Act." Katie Coyle and Nadiene Van Dyke have noted that many of the madams of Storyville were lesbians or at least bisexual.[39]

Coyle and Van Dyke situate their analysis of lesbianism in Storyville in comparison to lesbianism at Newcomb College, a private educational institution for "proper young ladies"—in other words, the daughters of the affluent white men who patronized Storyville.

Storyville lasted from 1897 to 1917. Despite the lingering Victorianism of this era, with all its notions of sexual purity and class distinctions, the zeitgeist at the turn of the century was more progressive than modern readers may suppose. We tend to think of this period as being completely closed-minded, but there were voices for sexual liberation. One such voice came from an unlikely place—a church pulpit in New Orleans. It wasn't until 2019, when Jonathan Ned Katz published his research, that Carl Schlegel became a name known to queer historians. At the turn of the century, New Orleans boasted one of the earliest, if not the earliest, voices for LGBT+ equality. In March 1905, a German Presbyterian church in New Orleans welcomed its new pastor, the Reverend Carl Schlegel (1863–1922). Born in Germany in 1863, Schlegel attended seminary in New Jersey and pastored a church in Manhattan before coming to New Orleans. His pastorate lasted under two years, and he was deposed in 1907. His sin? Publicly advocating for the decriminalization of homosexuality. The Presbytery of New Orleans charged him with having and preaching heretical views regarding homosexuality, alleging he "holds, maintains, disseminates and defends the naturalness and lawfulness of Sodomy, otherwise called 'Homosexuality' or 'Uranism.'"[40] Katz, who published his research in *OutHistory,* describes Schlegel as "one of the earliest U.S. homosexual emancipation activists."[41] In addition to preaching decriminalization in his church, Schlegel was also active in the Scientific-Humanitarian Committee, a queer advocacy group based in Germany. Another member of that group, Henry Gerber, founded the Society for Human Rights in Chicago in 1924.[42]

If sexual identity and notions of gender are socially constructed, there was very little construction going on prior to the advent of gay bars in New Orleans. The closet was not only a linguistic metaphor but also a very real, very invisible space. Much has been written about the burgeoning gay communities of New York and San Francisco at the turn of the twentieth century, but queerness in New Orleans has been largely ignored among gay historians. The closet in New Orleans remained quiet and crowded. Considering the fact there isn't a lot of source material to work with and, to a lesser extent, a subtle anti-southern bias exists in much of American historiography, the neglect of New Orleans in American gay history narratives is somewhat explainable, if regrettable.

One thing New York, San Francisco, and New Orleans have in common is they are all ports of entry to the United States for international visitors and immigrants. As major ports, all three cities host large, transient populations. Gay historians have long noted the effect of such demographics on the gay community. Charles Kaiser, for example, argues in *The Gay Metropolis* that the modern gay liberation movement in the United States can be traced to the enlisted men who traveled the globe in World War II: "People from all over the country who had assumed that they were unique learned that they were not alone. Soldiers and sailors also got a chance to sample gay culture all over the world—and discovered that large gay communities already existed in American ports of entry like San Francisco and New York City."[43]

Kaiser does not mention a gay community in New Orleans perhaps because, unlike New York or San Francisco, gay life in New Orleans was not concentrated in a specific neighborhood. In the opening years of the twentieth century, San Francisco had its Tenderloin District and New York had its Greenwich Village, but New Orleans had no such gayborhood. In the present day, we can point to the Marigny and lower Quarter as "gay zones," but at the dawn of the century, the Marigny was home to a low-income, working class of people, and the Quarter was essentially a run-down slum housing mostly Sicilian immigrants.

In the nineteenth century, sections of the Quarter were well-established "sex zones." As was the case in most port cities, the waterfront was where many sex workers congregated. Gallatin Street running along the French Market was particularly seedy. Lucy J. Fair observes the waterfront entertained "an unusually high number of Greek seafarers . . . Such Greek bars even today remain heavily mixed, straight and gay."[44] In the early twentieth century, Storyville, which was adjacent to the French Quarter, was the city's primary red-light district, although lower Canal Street and the Exchange Place Alley area was also the working domain of many sex workers. When Storyville was shut down in 1917, many brothels and sex workers migrated into the upriver, lakeside corner of the Quarter in a district known as "the Tango Belt."[45]

THE PRESERVATIONISTS

Some queer figures from the early twentieth century who made significant contributions to the city are remembered for their cultural impacts, but often those who know their names today do not know they were queer. This is certainly true of the gay men who advocated for the preservation of the French Quarter: Lyle Saxon, Allison Owen, Richard Koch, and William R. Irby. Were it not for these gay men, the French Quarter today might not exist.

When Saxon (1891–1946) arrived in New Orleans from Baton Rouge in 1917, the French Quarter was a run-down slum housing mostly working-class immigrants. The riverfront, so visitor friendly and picaresque today, was then all wharves and docks and stevedores and shipping activity. Decatur Street was a rough stretch that catered to sailors, dock workers, and transients. Before the T-shirt and daiquiri shops, Decatur was bars and brothels. But Saxon saw past all the debauchery and decrepit buildings and envisioned the neighborhood as an artistic haven.

Saxon, a successful journalist and writer, promoted the Quarter tirelessly. Not only was he a leader in encouraging its architectural preservation; he was also instrumental in attracting writers and artists to the deteriorating neighborhood. In his biography of Saxon, James Thomas writes, "Gradually, Tallant concludes, the French Quarter—primarily because of Saxon's influence—became 'more an art colony, less an underworld.'"[46] In fact, an easy argument can be made that Saxon single-handedly saved the Quarter from sure ruin and ultimate destruction. Saxon became known around town as "Mr. New Orleans" and eventually headed the Louisiana Writers Project, a part of President Franklin Roosevelt's Works Progress Administration (WPA). The result of that monumental effort was *Gumbo Ya-Ya: Louisiana Folktales* (1945).[47]

Saxon's work as a preservationist can be traced to 1919, when fire destroyed the old French Opera House.[48] Located at the corner of Bourbon and Toulouse Streets, the French Opera House was built in 1859 and served as the epicenter of Creole culture for a half-century. When Saxon learned the venerable old building was on fire, he rushed to the scene and wept. In his newspaper column the following day, he wrote, "The heart of the old French Quarter stopped beating yesterday."[49] Later Saxon restored properties on both Royal and Madison Streets.

While Saxon played a pivotal role in the Quarter's evolution from slum to artists' enclave in the early twentieth century, a number of other gay men began advocating for the protection and preservation of the neighborhood. At that time, the French Quarter was in danger of being torn down to make way for modern development. In 1895, the city council authorized the demolition of the Cabildo. Fronting Jackson Square next to St. Louis Cathedral, the Cabildo was one of the oldest buildings in the Lower Mississippi Valley, having been constructed in the 1790s. Now part of the Louisiana State Museum, it originally served as the seat of government during the Spanish colonial period. Paperwork for the Louisiana Purchase in 1803 was signed there, and the building's historical significance cannot be overstated. The fact that the city authorized its destruction is astonishing to modern readers, but at the fin de siècle, historical preservation was not really on many people's minds, except for a few gay men.

Fighting the effort to destroy the Cabildo was a gay man named Allison Owen (1869–1951). Colonel Owen led the famed New Orleans based Washington Artillery in World War I before he was promoted to the rank of brigadier general. Owen studied architecture at the Massachusetts Institute of Technology and later cofounded the architectural firm Diboll & Owen. The former military man turned architect would go on to also preserve what is now known as the Beauregard-Keyes House, a beautiful, rare example of Greek Revival architecture in the French Quarter, as well as build other landmarks throughout the city such as the Pythian Temple and Notre Dame Seminary.

The historic preservation bell was sounded again when the entire 400 block between Chartres and Royal Streets was destroyed in 1909 to make way for what is now the Supreme Court building. Upon completion, local residents hated the Beaux Arts style building because it was so out of scale for the neighborhood. Historians decried the loss of part of Exchange Place Alley, which ran from Canal Street to the front of the old St. Louis Hotel (now the Omni Orleans). The demolition of the old St. Louis Hotel in 1917 also raised pres-

Writer and preservationist Lyle Saxon, 1921. Anna Wynne Watt and Michael D. Wynne Jr. Collection, The Historic New Orleans Collection, acc. no. 1979.210.3.

ervation awareness. The modern tourism industry, which depends so much on the "old-world charm" of the French Quarter, was not yet born. The Vieux Carré Commission (VCC) was still years away. It was into this milieu that gay men began restoring and saving historic properties.

Chief among those gay men was architect Richard Koch (1889–1971). Like Saxon, Koch worked with the Works Progress Administration (WPA) in the Historic American Buildings Survey (HABS). Koch graduated from Tulane University with a degree in architecture in 1910 and then studied in Paris, before working for a few firms in the Northeast. He then returned to New Orleans. Upon returning home, Koch quickly established himself as a pioneer in "rescue architecture" and a leader in the emerging field of architectural preservation. He worked closely with Elizabeth Werlein to establish the Vieux Carré Commission. Some of his firm's early work projects included the restoration of Shadows on the Teche, a plantation home in New Iberia owned by a gay man named Weeks Hall, who also lived in New Orleans, as well as Oak Alley in Vacherie. And when Le Petit Théâtre moved to the French Quarter (at Lyle Saxon's urging), it was Koch who designed the playhouse building. Other French Quarter buildings Koch worked on that modern readers may be familiar with include the B-K House, Madame John's Legacy, the Hermann-Grima House, the Girod House (now known as the Napoleon House), and Lafitte's Blacksmith Shop (the original home of Café Lafitte).

Of Koch's early work, Julie H. McCollum writes, "His firm's restorations helped increase awareness of the need for historic preservation and spark a renaissance of cultural activity in New Orleans's French Quarter."[50] Part of that "cultural activity" was the creation of the Arts and Crafts Club, of which Koch was a cofounder in 1919. Originally called the "Artists Guild," the club introduced contemporary artistic influences and movements to New Orleans as well as sponsored traveling exhibitions, lectures, and classes for emerging artists.[51] The group initially met in Alberta Kinsey's small apartment at the corner of St. Peter Street and Cabildo Alley, before moving around the corner to Martha Westfeldt's fabled Green Shutter Tea Room (just a few doors down from Lyle Saxon's home).[52] In 1921, the Arts and Crafts Club found a suitable home at 520 Royal Street when gay philanthropist William Ratcliffe Irby renovated the rear part of his home and donated its use to the club.

William Ratcliffe Irby (1860–1926) was yet another gay preservationist. Irby, who moved to New Orleans as a child, was a wealthy tobacco executive and banker and also served as president of Tulane University's board of administrators. With his fortune, and his connections, Irby began advocating for the preservation of the city's flagship neighborhood. In 1915, when a Category 4 hurricane ravished New Orleans, Irby donated $125,000 to the Roman Catholic Archdiocese to repair the damage St. Louis Cathedral had sustained during the storm. Irby also rescued the French Opera House in 1913, when it was struggling financially and was forced into receivership.[53] Irby purchased the building and donated it to Tulane University. Another building Irby saved was 417 Royal Street, the current site of Brennan's restaurant. Built in 1795, by 1805 it was home to the Bank of Louisiana, the first bank opened in New Orleans after the Louisiana Purchase. It would later become the home of World Chess champion Paul Morphy, who died there in 1884. In 1920, Irby donated the building to Tulane University, which leased the property in 1954 to Owen Brennan. The Brennan family purchased the building in 1984. Yet another notable building Irby restored was the Seignouret-Brulatour House at 520 Royal Street. The property would later serve as the headquarters of WDSU-TV from 1950 to 1966. It is now owned by the Historic New Orleans Collection.

But of all Irby's restoration projects, perhaps the most notable is the lower Pontalba Building, which flanks the St. Ann side of Jackson Square. The Pontalba buildings, block-long row houses, are named after the woman who built them in the late 1840s, the fabled Baroness Micaela Almonester de Pontalba. By the early 1900s, the buildings had fallen into disrepair and were essentially tenements for poor immigrants. In 1921, Irby purchased the entire building for $68,000 from Pontalba's grandson and bequeathed it to the Louisiana State Museum, which still owns it today. The cast iron adorning the building's galleries are what set the trend for cast iron in New Orleans. The careful observer will notice embedded in the ironwork a series of cartouches, each featuring a monogram with the letters *A* (for the maiden name Almonester) and *P* (for the married name Pontalba). Hilary Irvin has noted that Pontalba's son Gaston—who achieved some fame as an artist and who was gay—"may have designed the 'AP' monograph adorning the buildings' cast-iron verandas"—an early example of a gay man setting a trend, as it were, at least architecturally.[54]

Owen, Irby, Koch, and Saxon were the first in a long line of gay men who have served as guardians of New Orleans architecture. Subsequent generations would see the likes of Boyd Cruise, Arnold Genthe, Clay Shaw, Curt Greska, Lloyd Sensat, Gene Cizek, Randy Plaisance, Larry Hesdorffer, and Bryan Block.

In the 1920s, Irby, along with Saxon, became a part of what John Shelton Reed calls the "Dixie Bohemia"—a circle of writers and artists and like-minded friends in the French Quarter who would play a vital role in transforming the Quarter from a run-down slum on the verge of being razed into a viable neighborhood that not only fostered creativity but was also worth preserving. Other gay (and bisexual) men who played a role in this transformation included Weeks Hall (artist), Sam Gilmore (poet and playwright), William Spratling (Tulane professor and silversmith), Pops Whitesell (photographer), and Cicero Odiorne (photographer).[55]

FRENCH QUARTER RENAISSANCE

At the center of this Dixie Bohemia was Lyle Saxon, who served as the impetus for what has subsequently been described as the "French Quarter Renaissance" of the 1920s. Saxon knew that to be in New Orleans is to step outside of time and enter a world of dreams and letters, a world perfumed by jasmine and oleander with the faintest hint of mud scent wafting in from the Mississippi, a world where people move slowly, aware of but unconcerned with time. He knew that in New Orleans, especially in the Quarter, myth and reality meld to form a dreamy realm where imagination reigns supreme and care is wholly abandoned. For artists and dreamers, the city itself is a poem. New Orleans has been described as the longest-running literary salon in America, and it really is true. Andrei Codrescu writes of New Orleans: "I had the fleeting thought that everyone, dead or alive, returns to New Orleans. If people can't come back in their lifetimes, they come back when they are dead. And everyone who ever lived here, the costumed French and Spanish dandies, the Victorian ladies of Kate Chopin's age, the whores and ruffians, and the poets, are still here. In a city like New Orleans, built for human beings in the age before cars, it's possible to move about the streets with ease and there is plenty of room for everyone."[56]

Albert Einstein famously observed imagination was more important than knowledge. What he meant is that knowledge is often conjured from imagination. Such was certainly the case in his famous thought experiments. He imagined what it would be like to travel at the speed of light, and when he quit daydreaming, humanity had a revolutionary new understanding of physics and the universe and our place in it.

But imagination spawns much more than knowledge; from imagination springs art and music and literature and food, to say nothing of hopes and dreams and the occasional nightmare. If there was ever a place on earth that embraces imagination and the creativity it engenders, that place is New Orleans. It is no wonder jazz and gumbo were born here or that no other American city has an entire season dedicated to creativity and fantasy (Carnival). It is no wonder the streets here are named after writers and musicians and mythological figures, including all the Muses. More than one observer has described New Orleans as a far-flung outpost of the Hellenistic world; it is no surprise, therefore, the Muses feel at home in this New World Mount Parnassus. Their interplay charges the atmosphere with creativity and fills the air with inspiration.

Lyle Saxon knew it and preached it, redeeming and transforming the Quarter in the process. In so doing, he in effect carved out a "gay space" in a city where no such space previously existed. An early, tangible manifestation of that space was Café Lafitte. Eventually, the bar would become the loci of the gay gentrification of the lower Quarter. Saxon's legacy lives on not only in the Quarter but also in the neighboring Marigny, for he bequeathed his passion for preservation to future generations of gay men. The gay men who revitalized the Marigny in the 1970s and 1980s may rightfully claim Saxon's mantle, and he would certainly approve of the Marigny's bohemian character. In "The Gay Penchant for Preservation," Will Fellows explores what drives the extraordinary gay male penchant for preservation: "The typical facile explanations tend to revolve around things like gay men's disposable income, childlessness, social oppression and marginalization. In reality, I discovered a rather consistent pattern comprising five key traits—Gender Atypicality, Domophilia, Romanticism, Aestheticism, and Connection."[57]

Fellows's analysis rings true: "A deep domesticity," "relating to the past in imaginative and emotional ways," "a relationship to the lives . . . who have gone before"—do not all these characteristics emanate from a profound yearning for belonging? This yearning is a ghost that hauntingly defined what it meant to be gay in pre-Stonewall America, and it's a specter that is still conjured every time a young schoolboy realizes he is "different." Thanks to Saxon and those who inherited his vision, it's a phantom that is nowhere near as scary as it used to be.

The creation of gay enclaves within larger cities certainly has its advantages for the gay community, namely safe and visible spaces for gays to be themselves; however, the gay neighborhood may also have its disadvantages. Some sociologists have questioned the value of safe spaces for minority populations. Exploring the African American experience, Farah Jasmine Griffin writes of "ghettos": "At their most progressive . . . spaces of retreat, healing and resistance; at their most reactionary . . . potentially provincial spaces which do not encourage resistance but instead help create complacent subjects whose only aim is to exist within the confines of the power that oppresses them."[58]

Is Griffin's warning applicable to the "gayification" of the lower Quarter and Marigny? Yes and no. At the time, gays had accepted their oppression as a sad fact of life. Resistance was a difficult concept to grasp, and given the zeitgeist in which they found themselves, just having a "gay" area was a giant leap forward.

PROHIBITION

January 16, 1920, was a dark day for bars in the United States. That was the day America outlawed alcohol. For thirteen years, serving or drinking alcohol meant violating the U.S. Constitution. New Orleans for the most part simply ignored Prohibition. Local authorities turned a blind eye as wine, liquor, and beer flowed freely in bars and restaurants throughout the city. Of course, some bars disappeared, never to resurface. But many bars remained in operation, even if barely underground. The Old Absinthe House didn't even bother to go underground. Speakeasies were ubiquitous, homemade hooch was all the rage, and New Orleans remained, by far, the wettest city in the country during the reign of the Volstead Act, the federal law that spelled out how Prohibition was to be enforced. Prohibition in New Orleans? Not so much.

Federal authorities were not amused. In 2008, the *New Orleans Times-Picayune* published an article commemorating the seventy-fifth anniversary of the end of Prohibition in which journalist Todd A. Price noted: “In 1923, federal authorities sent their best undercover agent here to dry up the oceans of illegal alcohol still flowing. Isidor Einstein, a self-promoting ‘master of disguise’ known nationwide as Izzy, arrived in New Orleans looking for booze. He found it moments later, when a cab driver offered to sell him a pint.”[59] For the next ten days, Izzy put together a list of more than eight hundred people violating the Volstead Act. Agents spent a week raiding speakeasies and arresting bootleggers. The *Times-Picayune* noted that when this offensive ended and the weekend arrived, liquor “flowed freely,” seats at “thronged” cabarets were nearly impossible to find, and “a number of old-timers declared New Orleans nightlife Saturday rivaled that of pre-Volsteadian days.”[60]

Prohibition in New Orleans was widely regarded as a colossal annoyance. When it ended, the city rejoiced as if it was Mardi Gras. John Magill, who has written extensively about that era of New Orleans history, observes:

> At noon on April 13, 1933, beverages containing 3.2 percent alcohol were legalized by Congress. The *Times-Picayune* reported, “New Orleans can have a jubilant legal whoopee party . . . the skyscrapers will be a-rocking and a-reeling before midnight.” There were 911 retail beer permits issued in the city within a few days; restaurants became beer gardens, and hotel bars reopened. Everyone waited with great restraint until noon when sirens wailed and crowds cheered. Convoys of beer trucks stretched for blocks, Canal Street was thronged with merrymakers, and 488,000 gallons of beer were sold in a few hours. The *Times-Picayune* stated that “there had not been so spontaneous an outpouring of joyous citizenry since the Armistice.”[61]

At best, the Feds were a nuisance to New Orleans, a city that has never fully trusted “the Americans” to begin with. According to legend, when Louisiana was transferred from France to the United States in 1803, the American flag got stuck as it was being hoisted up the pole in the Place d’Armes. True or not, the image is prophetic, for American mores such as the Protestant work ethic and Puritanical morality never truly took root in this far-flung French and Spanish outpost of European civilization. Besides, the enslaved people who built the city had their own culture and customs, which were allowed to flourish here. Stiff-upper-lip British stoicism and industriousness, so successfully imported to New England, never had a chance in New Orleans.

Well into the twentieth century, the city was divided into Creole and American sections, with Canal Street being the dividing line. In the nineteenth century, there were even separate municipalities. Even today, New Orleans remains the most un-American city in America, a distinction often noted by visitors. When the Louisiana Purchase happened, the native New Orleanians were surprisingly ambivalent, if not hostile, about their new status as Americans. By 1803, New Orleans had been founded by the French, acquired by the Spanish, turned over to France again, and infused with immigrants from all over Europe. Throw in involuntary immigration from several regions in Africa, and you have a societal mentality that never bought into, and still to this day resists, Anglo-Saxon Protestantism, with all its oppressive morality and mistrust of monarchy and laborious work ethic and bland food. The late great A. J. Liebling had it right when he observed that "New Orleans is within the orbit of a Hellenistic world that never touched the North Atlantic."[62] And it's true. Even now, it's easy to distinguish between visitors from Europe and, say, Missouri or Ohio. Visitors from Spain or Italy or Greece look completely at ease; visitors from America's heartland look like freshmen on the first day of fall classes.

New Orleans has always been a drinking town. Alcohol was a leading import for most of the colonial period. Home brewing was popular too; in 1802, 100,140 empty bottles were imported to the city. New Orleans's first city tax was a tax on billiard tables and taverns. That was a profitable move; the 1791 census indicates half of all the merchants in the city were tavern keepers.

Long before the French arrived with their penchant for "passing a good time," the Indigenous people who occupied South Louisiana were having a good time of their own. Of the First Nation inhabitants, Nancy Friedman observes: "Native Americans indulged in elaborate dances, spirited gambling, stickball games . . . Europeans adopted these and added billiards, duels, promenades and horse racing."[63] This happy marriage of multicultural hedonism multiplied over the centuries, with a plenitude of cultures and ethnicities each making its own intemperate contribution, and continues to this day. Among them are a wide variety of Indigenous people, French, Spanish, Swiss, German,

Senegalese, Gambian, Angolans, Congolese, Haitian, Cuban, German, Irish, Chinese, Sicilian, Croatians, Vietnamese, and Hondurans.

In the eighteenth century, public balls were held twice a week and were attended by virtually everyone. French colonial governor Pierre de Rigaud de Vaudreuil de Cavagnial (1698–1778), a man of impeccable taste with a charming personality, is credited with introducing balls and other social events to New Orleans in the 1740s, a move that won him favor with the populace. He also turned a blind eye to smuggling, which allowed the black market to thrive, which also helped his popularity.[64] Public balls featured dancing, eating, drinking, and gambling.

So important were these weekly balls to French New Orleans that when France ceded Louisiana to Spain, one of the primary concerns, in addition to the economic implications of the transfer of state, was whether or not the Spanish Crown would discontinue the weekly parties. The French colonists took no chances. The insurrection of 1768 resulted in the deportation of the first Spanish colonial governor, Antonio de Ulloa. The rebellion was crushed the following year, and New Orleans came firmly under Spanish sovereignty. The five leaders of the uprising were executed on the edge of town where Frenchmen Street meets Esplanade Avenue. The street was named in their honor.

The man who squashed the French rebellion was an Irish mercenary in service to the Spanish Crown named Alexander O'Reilly. At this time, the city, not yet a half-century old, had already earned a reputation as a drinking town. During his short tenure as colonial governor, O'Reilly instituted a number of reforms, including "limiting the number of drinking establishments in New Orleans, which had gained a reputation for its high number of rowdy taverns. By proclamation of October 8, 1769, O'Reilly allowed twelve taverns, six billiard halls, and one limonadier (lemonade vendor) to serve alcoholic beverages. The regulation prohibited criminals, vagabonds, and prostitutes from frequenting these establishments, and it forbade the use of swear words and blasphemy."[65] By the time of the Louisiana Purchase, New Orleans had well established itself as a party town and maintained a detached indifference to whatever flag was flying in Jackson Square.

So, if New Orleans has resisted American/Protestant values so successfully, why has its queer past remained so closeted? One easy answer is the Roman

Catholic Church. Make no mistake about it—at its core, New Orleans is a Catholic city. And while Roman Catholicism is relatively permissive compared to its Protestant counterparts, it has always towed the line on homosexuality. If the Catholic Church didn't condemn homosexuality so venomously, it is reasonable to assume most New Orleanians would have adopted a less harsh attitude toward gayness—out of sight, out of mind; don't ask, don't tell, so to speak. But there is another reason local queer history remains so hidden.

When the queer community in New Orleans began to inch the closet door open, the tourism industry was developing, and the power establishment (government and business leaders) that ran the city feared queer visibility would scare off tourist dollars. The money generated by tourism provided a strong incentive to keep gays and lesbians in the closet.[66] That gay people had plenty of money to spend never occurred to the city at the time. The spending power of the gay community wasn't realized until the late 1990s and 2000s, in no small part due to the economic impact of Southern Decadence—the Labor Day weekend extravaganza that grew exponentially after the advent of the internet. How the city aggressively suppressed queer visibility in the French Quarter is discussed in detail in a later chapter.

To be sure, the law also hindered tolerance. Before and after Prohibition, a city ordinance harking back to O'Reilly's reforms forbade bar owners from serving "degenerates"; doing so could result in a police raid. Gay bars, as we know them now, did not—indeed, could not—legally exist. After the repeal of the Volstead Act, few brave bars, however, welcomed gays. One such bar was Café Lafitte, located on the corner of Bourbon and St. Philip Streets.

McDonogh, Whitman, Reizenstein, Jackson, Schlegel; the lesbian and bisexual sex workers in Storyville; and Saxon and the lives of the queer preservationists demonstrate the incredible contributions gay men were making to New Orleans in the decades before gay bars existed. They were here. They were queer. But they had no place to drink—at least not a place where they could truly be themselves. That would change in 1933.

2

Café Lafitte Before the Exile

LAFITTE'S BLACKSMITH SHOP

As New Orleans emerged from the dark days of Prohibition, the French Quarter was a much different neighborhood than it had been prior to the Volstead Act. In the years between the world wars, the district was still essentially residential, although the seeds of the now booming tourist economy had been planted. The riverside edge of the Quarter was still dominated by the shipping industry and the attendant businesses that come with any busy port—ship chandleries, saloons, gambling dens, and brothels. Among the Quarter's working class, mostly Sicilian immigrants, there were pockets of affluence, primarily along Royal Street. There was also a small Chinatown along Bourbon Street. The entertainment district of Bourbon Street was beginning to take shape but had not yet coalesced into the neon strip we know today.

A small yet influential literati also thrived in the Quarter. Writers and artists and others interested in preservation recognized something special in the dilapidated neighborhood and forged a genuine community. Literary salons and artist studios flourished, as did the performing and visual arts at places such as Le Petit Théâtre and the Arts and Crafts Club. *The Double-Dealer,* an important Modernist literary journal that published the likes of Ernest Hemingway, William Faulkner, and Ezra Pound, emerged out of this setting, and journalists from New York began describing the French Quarter as a bohemian's paradise, a southern Greenwich Village. In addition to the regular local

Café Lafitte in the 1940s. Collins C. Diboll Vieux Carré Digital Survey, The Historic New Orleans Collection, N-144.

characters, a steady flow of writers from elsewhere came through to soak up the atmosphere as well, among them Gertrude Stein, Alice B. Toklas, John Dos Passos, Carl Carmer, and Edna St. Vincent Millay.

This intelligentsia was a community within a community and included not only writers and artists but also socialites and newspaper columnists who published regularly about the "Quarter scene." Famed novelist Sherwood Anderson lived in the upper Pontalba building at the time with his wife, Elizabeth, who recalled their time living in the French Quarter as "social and congenial."[1] By the early 1930s, the French Quarter was a demimonde in the truest sense of the word, and everyone seemed to know each other. Queerness within the group was common but unimportant to those within the circle, despite pressure from the heteronormative paradigm of the outside world. Somehow the Quarter was a place where the rest of society's rules just didn't apply.[2]

In this environment, it was inevitable that a bar like Café Lafitte would emerge and thrive. In 1933, shortly after the repeal of the Volstead Act, Tom Caplinger, Harold Bartell, and Mary Collins leased the building at 941 Bourbon Street (at the corner of St. Philip Street) and opened a bar called Café Lafitte. Caplinger's daughter remembers her father falling in love with the building when he first saw it. At the time, it was just one of two bars on Bourbon Street, the other being the Old Absinthe House. Contrary to popular belief, the iconic building at 941 Bourbon had never housed a bar before then.

Café Lafitte was an instant hit. The physical appearance of the building—the worn-away plaster, the exposed wood and ancient bricks, the fact it was leaning slightly—immediately established an old and mysterious atmosphere, a mystique underscored by the name Lafitte, with all its romantic and roguish connotations. The central fireplace anchored the cozy space, which at night was illuminated by candles, underscoring its historical associations. Paintings from local artists adorned the walls, and the bar was filled with locals from the neighborhood. It was not uncommon to spot a national celebrity in the bar enjoying a slice of authentic French Quarter life. Laughter erupted frequently as the bartenders regaled the regulars with ribald tales of drunken adventures. It was a warm, welcoming place.

The building today housing Lafitte's Blacksmith Shop bar dates to roughly 1772 and was built by a man named Nicolas Touze.[3] It is historically significant not only architecturally but also because it is one of just a few buildings that survived two great fires that destroyed the original city in the late 1700s. The Good Friday Fire of 1788 consumed 856 buildings, and the fire of 1794 resulted in the loss of 212 buildings. After those two fires, the Spanish, under whose dominion Louisiana was at the time, instituted a building code, commonly referred to as a "fire code." This code stipulated buildings be constructed flush up against the street (no front yards), wells be dug in rear courtyards (today's beautiful fountains), and exposed wood be covered by stucco or plaster. For this reason, the Spanish are very much responsible for the way the French Quarter looks today; however, it would be inaccurate to say the architecture in the French Quarter is predominantly Spanish. In fact, most of the buildings in the neighborhood today were constructed between 1820 and 1850, with a plurality being built in the 1830s.

The Blacksmith Shop at 941 Bourbon Street is today widely considered to be the oldest building used as a bar in the United States.[4] It is one of the most photographed buildings in the French Quarter because of its age and unique appearance. The architectural style of the building is old French Provincial Louis XV, or *briquette-entre-poteaux,* common in Louisiana under French rule. The Vieux Carré Commission notes, "Its steep hipped roof is reminiscent of French provincial thatched roof cottages and is part of a design that probably came to New Orleans via French Canada."[5] The lot on which it stands was originally granted to Jean Cossine in 1722, shortly after the street grid of the fledgling city was laid out. It was then regranted to Nicolas Touze, who by 1732 constructed a house facing St. Philip Street. In 1771, the property was owned by Jean Baptiste Laporte and his wife, Domenica. The Laporte's son-in-law was Captain Renato Beluche, one of Jean Lafitte's Baratarians, who assisted Lafitte in aiding the Americans at the Battle of New Orleans. In 1778, Beluche would purchase what is now known as Madame John's Legacy, another of the few buildings in New Orleans surviving from the eighteenth century.

Simon Duroche purchased the property in 1773 and owned it for sixty years. Colonial records indicate Duroche often used a fake name, "Castillon." Edith Long speculates the alias may have been necessary to conceal Duroche's involvement in illicit trade. She writes: "No record tells us what he did, but the alias smacks of adventure and enterprise. Throughout this period many New Orleanians dabbled in the ill-gotten gains of smuggling and piracy. The Lafittes boldly maintained a shop on Royal, and advertised in the local press when a fine auction was to be held from their warehouses at Barataria . . . If Duroche-Castillon was a blacksmith-pirate we have no way of knowing now."[6]

In 1833, the building was sold to Madame Christian Miltenberger, "widow of a surgeon in the Battle of New Orleans."[7] In 1838, Miltenberger would construct a row house nearby, at the corner of Dumaine and Royal Streets. It was here that Alice Heine, the first American princess of Monaco, was born. Dr. Miltenberger and his wife had emigrated from Alsace, France, to Saint-Domingue, where they owned coffee plantations. During the Saint-Domingue slave insurrection of the 1790s, they fled to New Orleans, where Dr. Miltenberger became an authority on yellow fever. The widow Miltenberger sold the cottage at 941 Bourbon to Hugh Dowlin in 1851.

It remained in the Dowlin family until 1885, when it was sold to John Langles, in whose family it remained until 1901. Property records list Clément Dabezies as the owner until 1913, at which time it was sold to John A. Barbe Sr. In 1933 Barbe leased the building to Tom Caplinger, who opened Café Lafitte. After Barbe's death, in 1953, the building was sold at auction to Bertrous G. Joseph, who leased the business to John T. Moore. By 1958, the building was owned by an entity called Lafitte's Blacksmith Shop, Inc.

The aforementioned chain of title and its attendant history illustrate the building's fascinating story and offer hints into how the Lafitte mythology surrounding the building may have arisen. Because of Renato Beluche's personal friendship with Jean Lafitte, it is reasonable to assume Lafitte knew the Laportes and may have spent time at their home on the corner of Bourbon and St. Philip Streets. Perhaps for this reason, it is commonly thought the Blacksmith Shop was a front for the pirate Jean Lafitte's smuggling operations in the city, but this is a myth propagated by fanciful tour guides. There is absolutely no evidence that this building was ever a Blacksmith Shop or that Jean Lafitte ever owned the property.[8]

The origin of the myth dates back to at least 1883. In that year, an article written by Lafcadio Hearn for *Century Magazine* references the property as "the famed smithy of the Brothers Lafitte."[9] Ten years later, Grace King and John Ficklen published *History of Louisiana,* which states, "The Lafittes, Pierre and Jean, came from France and opened a blacksmith shop in New Orleans on St. Philip Street."[10] Hearn, King, and Ficklen, however, provide no citation or other source material for this claim.

For most of its history, this building was a residence. Oddly, in *Old New Orleans: A History of the Vieux Carré,* which was published in 1936, Stanley Clisby Arthur writes, "From owner to owner the little house was transferred until it reached its present status—a plumber's shop."[11] This is puzzling because the building was housing the bar at this point. There is no indication it was a plumber's shop. The old cottage was a bar, and owner Tom Caplinger briefly lived in the attic with his family.

TOM CAPLINGER AND MARY COLLINS

Caplinger, who was straight, became something of a legend in the French Quarter not only as a brilliant bar owner but also for his generosity toward Quarterites, artists, writers, and anyone down on his luck. Roger "Tom" Caplinger

(1906–56) was originally from Maysville, Kentucky, where his dad served as superintendent of schools. Caplinger also lived in New York and Paris before settling in New Orleans. He worked as an actor, an interior decorator, and a model for a photographic essay called "A Day in the Life of a Bum During the Depression." He then became an antiques dealer, before purchasing the bar. Initially, Caplinger and his wife, Marion, and their four children were living above the bar, before later moving around the corner to 816 St. Philip. His daughter Grace Zabriskie grew up to be an accomplished actor and boasts film credits such as *Norma Rae* (1979), *Wild at Heart* (1990), and *Inland Empire* (2006) as well as television roles in *Twin Peaks, Santa Barbara, Seinfeld,* and the HBO series *Big Love.* In 2010, she published a book of poetry.

Under Caplinger's leadership, Café Lafitte earned an international reputation. In the 1940s, the consul general of France dubbed the bar "the Embassy of the Montmartre in New Orleans."[12] And in 1954, John Steinbeck wrote an article about Caplinger in the *Saturday Evening Post* in which he described Caplinger as "an uninhibited, unkempt scholar, whose laissez-faire policy of running a gin mill can only be termed unique."[13] The bar originally served food and played popular French music almost exclusively, at least until the local mafia, which controlled the jukebox business at the time, forced him to play popular American music. Caplinger was smart—both intellectually and streetwise—and he was also genuine. He really liked people, and that disposition is reflected in the bar's clientele. His daughter described the bar in a 1989 interview with Joe Frank, saying, "There were always artists and writers and performers of different kinds . . . it was like a Parisian café."

Much of Caplinger's success was due to his ability to connect with people. His daughter Grace recalls that he would often invite bar patrons to his house a block or so away and give them shirts or other articles of clothing they might need. She remembers, "He would bring people home from the Café at all hours of the night."[14] On some of these occasions, Caplinger would wake up Grace and have her recite T. S. Eliot or Shakespeare for their guests. He also supported artists and performers. He was particularly fond of a burlesque performer named Storme and would often take others to see her show a few blocks up Bourbon Street.

Rivaling Caplinger's charm and presence was co-owner Mary Collins (1901–67). Collins was born and raised in Algiers (the only part of New Orleans

Tom Caplinger, one of the original owners of Café Lafitte, n.d. From NewsBank database.

on the west bank of the river) and graduated from Newcomb College, before earning a master's degree in education from Tulane University. Collins lived in multiple locations in the French Quarter throughout her life, including residences on Royal, Bourbon, and Dauphine Streets. In addition to being a co-owner of Café Lafitte, she also worked as a clerk in the mayor's office during World War II.[15] Collins had a colorful personality fueled by copious amounts of scotch and an excessive love of cats. According to her friends, Tennessee Williams, who was a regular at Café Lafitte, used her typewriter to write his 1944 breakthrough masterpiece, *The Glass Menagerie.* Collins's father was a police officer, which has caused some to theorize this is why Caplinger brought her in as an owner in the bar, to preemptively avoid police harassment.

Many have claimed Collins was a lesbian. The fact is we just don't know. Fueling the speculation were Collins's choice of clothing and friends. Collins wore men's suits and had slicked-back hair. She was also friends with a number of queer people, most notably Dixie Fasnacht and Lyle Saxon. But to cite these observations as evidence of her sexuality would be circumstantial. The issue of Collins's sexuality matters somewhat in that it speaks to the question of what makes a gay bar gay. The owner(s)? The clientele? Both? Something else?

In April 1951, Collins, along with Bartell, sold her interest in Café Lafitte to

Mary Collins, one of the original owners of Café Lafitte, n.d. From NewsBank database.

a man named Lee Smith in order to try her hand in the real estate business.[16] A year later, Caplinger bought out Smith and ran the bar alone for a while.[17] Apparently, real estate didn't work out for Collins; by 1954, Collins and Bartell are listed in Thomas Griffin's popular gossip column as the owners (along with Caplinger) of the new Café Lafitte in Exile at 901 Bourbon Street.[18] This is the earliest written reference describing the bar at 941 Bourbon as "Lafitte's Blacksmith Shop." It is unclear how or when the rumor started that the property was once used by Jean Lafitte.[19] In the 1940s, Lyle Saxon and others described Café Lafitte as being located in "Lafitte's old blacksmith shop." Perhaps with marketing value on their minds, the three owners of the original bar never squashed the rumors that the famed pirate had once used the building as a front for his smuggling operation; conversely, a 1945 newspaper ad states: "CAFÉ LAFITTE—Bar in Lafitte's Old Blacksmith Shop—Since 1740."[20] How long the rumor had been circulating is a source of speculation and may have been why the owners chose the name Café Lafitte. Another explanation for the name may have to do with a 1930 book called *Lafitte the Pirate,* written by Lyle Saxon. Saxon, a friend of Collins, was a fanciful storyteller, and his book (and the Lafitte mythology) became so popular that Hollywood made a movie based on it—*The Buccaneer,* starring Errol Flynn.

Harold Bartell, one of the original owners of Café Lafitte, n.d. From NewsBank database.

Collins and Bartell would open another legendary bar in 1957, the Galley House at the corner of Chartres and Toulouse Streets. The Galley House would go on to earn a prominent place in the pantheon of lost gay bars in the French Quarter and would affectionately be called "The Wrinkle Room," because of the average age of its patrons. In the 1960s, Collins was the subject of two articles in national publications—*Life* magazine in 1961 and the *New Yorker* in 1965. She died in 1967. Funeral services were held at the tony Bultman Funeral Home and St. Louis Cathedral.[21] Collins, a devout Catholic, had once drunkenly called the Vatican to wish the pope Merry Christmas. The Vatican telephone operator diplomatically told Collins that His Holiness was unavailable but that she would relay the message.

The stories of Collins's life and escapades carousing in the Quarter are legion. Grace Zabriskie once remarked, "I don't think I ever saw her sober."[22] Zabriskie recalled once in an interview with Joe Frank having been chased around the courtyard by Collins, who was wielding a knife. Saxon devotes an entire chapter to Collins in his last work, *The Friends of Joe Gilmore* (1948). In it, he relates the story of how he and his valet Joe Gilmore popped into Dixie's Bar of Music for a nightcap when it was still located in the 200 block of St. Charles Avenue.[23] Dixie approached Saxon and said, "Our friend Miss

Mary is a little boxed, and I think you might take her home if you will." Saxon continues: "Mary Collins is one of the owners of the Café Lafitte, one of the most interesting of the French Quarter bars. It is in the old Blacksmith shop of Lafitte, the Pirate, and to call it highly picturesque is to make a very mild statement."[24]

Saxon continues: "So when Dixie asked that I take care of Mary, I realized that my task would be a delightful but difficult exploit. There was Mary walking around the tables, loving everybody and telling them so, except for a few whose faces did not appeal to her. As I went over to her, she was speaking to a Marine, who stood six feet four if he stood an inch, and she was saying: 'I wish you would go home; you are too big and too unattractive.'"[25]

Saxon coaxed Collins away from the marine and into his car, where Gilmore was waiting at the wheel, even though Collins made it clear she didn't want to leave. She suggested they go to another cocktail lounge, but Saxon and Gilmore convinced her a nice ride was in order.

> "Where do you live?" I asked, for Mary is constantly changing her place of abode. Sometimes she lives in Algiers across the Mississippi river, sometimes in uptown New Orleans on one of the fashionable thoroughfares; but more frequently she lives in the French Quarter.
>
> "How I wish it were Mardi Gras," she said.
>
> "Why?" I asked.
>
> "Then I could wear my traditional beard."
>
> "But it isn't Mardi Gras; it is nearly Easter."
>
> "Can't we go to an Easter egg hunt?"
>
> "Mary, where do you live?"
>
> "Guess."[26]

A long guessing game ensued, and they finally arrived at Collins's home in the 900 block of Royal Street, where Saxon and Gilmore tucked her into bed.

Collins's friends could be just as wild, and they fit right in at Café Lafitte. Consider the case of Captain George Tchakiris, a Greek merchant marine who frequented the bar when he was in port and regaled the regulars with tall tales of his exploits at sea. One anecdote in particular illustrates Collins's freewheeling spirit and carefree attitude as well as her generosity. The captain and a friend named Pepe had gone out on the town and ended up at a brothel. As they prepared to leave after a night of debauchery, they realized they had no money. Pepe recounts:

> "Pepe," ordered George. "Call Mary Collins at Lafitte."
>
> I did.
>
> "Mary," whined George. "We're in trouble, Pepe and me. We got to drinking and we went to this place . . . I hate to say this in front of you but . . . you know . . . this bawdy house . . . you know, this place where they have girls, and Mary, we're broke. They won't give us our clothes. Will you send Martin (the porter–assistant bartender) out with a hundred dollars? Please . . . Mary . . . it's so embarrassing . . . We'll pay you back as soon as I can get to my apartment."
>
> Mary, of course, was laughing hysterically by now . . . and she sent Martin with the hundred . . . or she started to. We called back and stopped her . . . said they took pity on us . . . and ended the "night" with a noon "nightcap" back at the café.[27]

Less is known of Harold Bartell, other than he lived uptown on Coliseum Street and that he played the piano. Bartell and Collins for a brief time owned a modified Creole cottage at 933–935 Bourbon Street (in the same block as the bar), which they purchased in 1947. It is unclear if they lived there or utilized it as a rental. Bartell sold his share of the building to Collins in 1951, who in turn sold hers the next year.

Judith Montagu, an aristocrat from England traveling through the United States in 1949, describes Bartell in her travel diary: "We then went on and had stingers at a place called Lafittes, a very dimly lit bar which used to be a blacksmith's shop kept by two pansies, one of whom played the piano very well . . . Mr. Griffiths, the lunch time queer, showed up, but there was a slight but noticeable froideur . . . One of the proprietors came in and sat at our table looking like a prize fighter, complete with broken nose, cauliflower ears and missing teeth, but talking in a series of high-pitched shrieks larded with 'my dears.'"[28]

He was apparently a figure of some note as he was mentioned regularly in newspapers' society columns. In 1949, the influential Arts and Crafts Club commissioned a portrait of him. In the same year, Bartell headed up a satellite version of Café Lafitte. The *New Orleans Item* reported, "Café Lafitte, the fabulous spot on lower Bourbon, is opening an 'uptown' branch a few blocks further up the street tonight with socialite Harold Barthel [*sic*] in charge; it'll be in the backstage room of Dan's International."[29] The "uptown" Lafitte's didn't last long. No mention of it is made in the papers after 1950, and no one we interviewed remembered it.

Caplinger, Collins, and Bartell were accepting of and welcoming to their gay clientele and offered them a safe place to drink and socialize. Although the bar could not be classified a "gay bar" as we think of that term today, it was as gay friendly as the times would permit. Mary Collins welcomed patrons enthusiastically and would often run tabs for people who had no cash. The bar had opened during the Great Depression, after all.

DRAMATIS PERSONAE

As one might expect, Café Lafitte was a trendy nightspot. Robert Kinney mentions the bar in his classic 1942 book, *The Bachelor in New Orleans,* suggesting, "If the bartender is passed out, go behind the bar and mix your own drink!"[30] In a city known for its bars, Café Lafitte was a must stop for visitors and a mecca for celebrities such as Lucius Beebe, Robert Mitchum, Jane Russell, Gore Vidal, Paul Douglas, Ernest Hemingway, Dwight Fiske, Kay Francis, and many others. In *My New Orleans,* local culinary legend Ella Brennan recalls the scene at Café Lafitte in the 1940s and 1950s: "Café Lafitte attracted all of the great talents in town. Tennessee Williams could be found there every night he was in town. You might run into the lead dancer for the Ballets Russes or a film star or actors in a hit play or the fabulous Mexican sculptor Enrique Alferez or politicians such as Hubert Humphrey and Eugene McCarthy or local politicos such as Earl Long and Chep Morrison or famous authors and syndicated journalists such as Robert Ruark."[31]

Contributing to the appeal of the bar were not only the colorful characters who patronized the place but also the personalities of the three proprietors. They deliberately fostered a welcoming environment in which stimulating conversation flowed easily, and the fun was contagious. For example, they would regularly invent new cocktails. Harold Bartell invented "Stromboli on the Rocks" in 1950, insisting the drink's ingredients were a secret but sardonically conceding that the rocks were ice. Caplinger's creation, "the Obituary," which consisted of a drop of absinthe added to a Manhattan, made the papers, as did yet another cocktail invented by Collins and Bartell.[32] Popular columnist Tom Griffin wrote: "A new type of Martini was whipped up by Mary Collins and Harold Bartell of Café Lafitte in Exile in honor of silver-tongued Clint Bolton's 40-odd birthday. It was a four to one deal with garlic rubbed on the inside of the glass as a sort of salad bowl. Clint's comment: 'Best Italian dinner I ever drank.'"[33]

Creative libations and clever conversation attracted a cross section of the Quarter's denizens to the bar. Some of the more interesting regulars included restauranteur Count Arnaud; sculptor Enrique Alferez; writers Tennessee Williams, Truman Capote and William March; and photographers Francis Benjamin Johnston and Pops Whitesell. Knowing a bit about these regular patrons gives us insight into the type of bar Café Lafitte was and the atmosphere it engendered.

Leon Bertrand Arnaud Cazenave (1876–1948) was born in the French village of Bosdarros, near the Pyrenees. After receiving his education in Paris, he came to the United States to study medicine. In order to earn money to pay for medical school, he became a French wine salesman, a job that brought him to New Orleans. Cazenave fell in love with New Orleans and settled in the city. He leased the Old Absinthe House and was running that business when he opened Arnaud's in 1918. The quality of Arnaud's French cuisine and its wine selection, coupled with Cazenave's charismatic personality, would win the restaurant accolades and earn it a place among the jewels of New Orleans's culinary crown. His daughter, Germaine Wells, eventually took stewardship of the restaurant and achieved legendary status herself. The Count, who was not really a count but liked to pretend he was, lived at 544 Esplanade Avenue. It is not difficult to imagine him popping into Café Lafitte on his way to and from the restaurant.

Enrique Alferez (1901–99) was born in Zacatecas, Mexico, and as a teenager worked as a mapmaker alongside Pancho Villa during the Mexican Revolution. In 1924, he enrolled at the Art Institute of Chicago, where he studied under the famous sculptor Lorado Taft. In 1929, he stopped in New Orleans on his way back to Mexico and fell in love with the city. The French Quarter particularly captivated him, and he remained in the city for the rest of his life. Upon settling there, he found work easily and also taught at the aforementioned Arts and Crafts Club as well as directing the sculpture program for the Works Progress Administration. His work today can be found throughout New Orleans, from the Central Business District to City Park to the Lakefront. Alferez's *Fountain of the Four Winds,* at the entrance of the Lakefront Airport, created something of a scandal when it was completed. WPA administrators and city officials objected to the male figure's rather well-endowed genitalia and ordered it removed. Alferez refused and threatened to shoot anyone who tried to chisel it off. Lyle Saxon and First Lady Eleanor Roosevelt ultimately intervened, and the piece was saved.[34]

The most famous regular to frequent the bar was playwright and screenwriter Tennessee Williams (1911–83). Born and raised in Mississippi, Williams eventually found fame and critical success with his play *The Glass Menagerie* (1944). In 1946, he wrote his next masterpiece, *A Streetcar Named Desire* (1947), while living in the French Quarter. Williams would live in the neighborhood on and off for the rest of his life. After *Streetcar,* Williams had a string of hits throughout the 1950s: *Summer and Smoke* (1948), *The Rose Tattoo* (1951), *Camino Real* (1953), *Cat on a Hot Tin Roof* (1955), *Orpheus Descending* (1957), *Garden District* (1958), and *Sweet Bird of Youth* (1959). Williams would eventually win numerous awards, including two Pulitzer Prizes and a Tony Award. Today he is regarded as one of the most significant playwrights of twentieth-century America.

In the French Quarter, Williams found a certain freedom that eluded him elsewhere. He would eventually call New Orleans his "spiritual home." Such a libertine environment allowed Williams's genius to flourish. Williams was a regular at both incarnations of Lafitte's and would eventually live only two blocks from the 901 Bourbon Street location. Tales of his exploits at the bar are legendary.

Yet another famous writer who frequented the bar when he was in town was novelist Truman Capote (1924–84), who was born in New Orleans and raised by his grandmother in Alabama. His breakthrough novel, *Other Voices, Other Rooms* (1948), is a gay bildungsroman and was followed by two other landmark works—*Breakfast at Tiffany's* (1958) and *In Cold Blood* (1966). He also wrote a plethora of short stories. Much of *Other Voices, Other Rooms* was writ-

Tennessee Williams in front of the LaBranche Building in 1977. The current proprietor of Café Lafitte in Exile now owns the building and maintains a residence there. The Historic New Orleans Collection, acc. no. 1994.143.4.

ten at an apartment he rented on Royal Street, just steps away from Tennessee Williams's apartment, around the corner on St. Peter Street. Capote reflected on the novel decades later in *The Dogs Bark* (1973): "*Other Voices, Other Rooms* was an attempt to exorcise demons, an unconscious, altogether intuitive attempt, for I was not aware, except for a few incidents and descriptions, of its being in any serious degree autobiographical. Rereading it now, I find such self-deception unpardonable."[35]

Although not as well-known as Williams and Capote, another accomplished writer who frequented Café Lafitte was William March (1893–1954). A marine who fought in World War I, March, like Capote, grew up in Alabama and would go on to publish over twenty short stories and a number of novels, including *Company K* (1933) and *The Bad Seed* (1954). In 1950, March moved to an apartment on Dumaine Street in the French Quarter, where he composed *The Bad Seed,* his most critically acclaimed work.

In addition to writers, Café Lafitte also attracted photographers, the most famous of whom was lesbian photographer Frances Benjamin Johnston (1864–1952), who lived only a block and a half from the bar. Born in the Victorian era during the Civil War, Johnston grew up in Washington, DC, then studied art in Paris. Upon returning to the States, she took up photography and blazed a trail in the young field for other lesbian photographers such as Clara Sipprell, Alice Austin, and later, Annie Leibovitz. Johnston quickly became one of the country's first female photojournalists, then shifted her focus to portraiture, opening her own studio. In addition to focusing on female nudes, something quite extraordinary for the time, she also began photographing celebrities, politicians, and members of Washington society, including five U.S. presidents. She then turned her lens to gardens and estates, before embarking on a remarkable project to document southern architecture pictorially. She also documented the lives of factory workers and African American students in the South, most notably at the Tuskegee Institute in Alabama.[36]

Johnston spent her time in the Quarter working, drinking, smoking, and socializing with friends, among whom was longtime Quarter eccentric and fellow photographer Joseph Woodson "Pops" Whitesell (1876–1958), also known as the "St. Peter Street Leprechaun" because of his diminutive stature.[37] Originally from Indiana, Whitesell moved to New Orleans in 1918 and quickly became a part of the artist's colony that had coalesced around Lyle Saxon.

Frances Benjamin Johnston and Pops Whitesell, ca. 1945–55. Gift of an Anonymous Donor, The Historic New Orleans Collection, acc. no. 2014.0198.1.40.

Whitesell achieved great success as a photographer; his work was exhibited throughout the world and purchased by a host of museums, including the Smithsonian Institution. He was awarded the title "master photographer" by the prestigious Professional Photographers Association, and he also boasted membership in the Photographic Society of America and Great Britain's Royal Photographic Society. Locally, he was the photographer of choice among the blue-blooded Uptown Carnival royalty, who probably had no idea he also contributed photographs for *Art & Physique,* a beefcake magazine popular with gay men at the time.[38]

In addition to the colorful, and famous, personalities who patronized Café Lafitte, another draw to the bar was that it served food, at least sometimes. In his 1938 classic book, *Dining in New Orleans,* Scoop Kennedy writes: "Food? Well, sometimes there is food. That is to say there are unpredictable periods when the cook locks the kitchen and stays away for six months. If you're hungry you had better 'phone and ask, 'Are you in the restaurant business today, please?'"[39] When food was being served, the menu included a choice of three or four entrées, including steaks, liver and onions, and roast beef. A complete dinner cost $1.75, although there was an upcharge for steaks. The kitchen was detached from the main building at the rear of the adjacent courtyard, which featured a large fig tree.[40] Seating was available at tiny tables in both the courtyard and inside the bar. Table service was provided by a server named Martin, described as elderly and dignified, unless patrons were seated at the oddly shaped bar, designed to reflect the curves in the Mississippi River as it flows past New Orleans. In the center of the room was a fireplace. On one wall, written in chalk, was the saying "Love makes time pass. Time makes love pass."

Caplinger, Bartell, and Collins ran an extremely popular bar that had in twenty years achieved the ambiance and reputation of much older bars from a grander age. Café Lafitte's popularity stemmed not only from the vibrant cast of characters who frequented the bar but also from the personality of its owners. Caplinger, Bartell, and Collins were genuinely good people—not something that can be said of all bar owners—but their generosity would eventually cost them the bar.

As noted, Café Lafitte freely ran bar tabs for those who had no money. Many of these tabs went unpaid, and when John Barbe, the owner of the building housing the bar, died, Caplinger, Bartell, and Collins could not afford to purchase the building, and Barbe's estate put the building up for auction. Several hundred people gathered to watch the auction, which was held in the bar's side patio. Caplinger was inside the bar with former manager Tony Devine when the bidding began. Caplinger and his business partners could not afford to purchase the building (the winning bid was $42,500), and when it sold, the bar closed for a few months.[41] When it reopened, under the new ownership of John T. Moore, the bar's gay clientele was no longer welcome.[42] Caplinger signed a lease on another building on the same block, opened another bar, and called it Café Lafitte in Exile. Years later, at the original bar, a box full of unpaid bar tabs was found, the sum of which would have easily paid for the building.

3

Post-Exile and the Closet

BOURBON AND DUMAINE

Café Lafitte in Exile opened in its current incarnation at 901 Bourbon Street in 1953. The early history of the building is something of a mystery. Early colonial records indicate the lot of ground on the downriver, lakeside corner of Bourbon and Dumaine Streets was initially granted to Jean Jarry, a "concession workman," and Louis Mechin.[1] By 1731, the lot was owned by someone called St. Germain (a name that Louis Mechin used as an alias).[2] In 1796, the lot was purchased by Mr. and Mrs. Blache, who owned it until 1829.[3] The Civil District Court Notarial Archives for Orleans Parish contain no records of transactions for the property between 1808 and the sheriff's sale, a public auction to satisfy a debt, in 1876. Based on the architecture, it is safe to assume the first floor of the building was constructed in the 1820s (probably as a corner store) and that the second floor was added at some point after the 1876 sheriff's sale. The Notarial Archives does not have a building contract on file for either the first floor or the later second-floor addition. By 1870, the property was owned by a "free man of color" named Etienne Cordeviolle.[4] Property records from 1876 suggest the property was sold at a sheriff's sale, but by 1883, the lot was back in the possession of the Cordeviolle family.

The first description of a building on the lot dates to 1883, when Ernest Cucullu took ownership: "together with a frame building, bricked between

Café Lafitte in Exile in the 1950s. Collins C. Diboll Vieux Carré Digital Survey, The Historic New Orleans Collection, N-234.

posts, of several rooms; two two-story brick buildings, built on the rear of the lot and fronting on Bourbon Street and containing several rooms, bricked yard, etc."[5] A Sanborn fire insurance map indicates the building was used as a saloon as early as 1908. For the balance of the twentieth century, 901 Bourbon went through a series of owners, until Tom Wood bought the property in 1994 for $510,000. It has functioned as a bar for at least 117 years.

At the turn of the century, the building at 901 Bourbon is listed in the city directories as both a saloon and a dry goods store.[6] The dry goods store may have been located behind the main building at 805 Dumaine Street. By 1918, that address is listed as housing the "Yakima Shaving Parlor."[7] In 1913, J. M. Senac opened the Yakima Saloon. During Prohibition, the saloon changed its name to the Yakima Social Club and described itself as a "soft drink stand," but it still served liquor. The club was raided twice in 1923. During the first raid, "Dry Enforcement Agents" confiscated "two gallons of gin, one gallon of whiskey and eighteen gallons of wine."[8] The business was sold in 1925 but remained a "soft drink stand" until 1928, when it became home to Nash Tailors.[9] In 1933, the year Prohibition was repealed, the Yakima Social Club relocated across the street, to 841 Bourbon, which would later become the Washing Well Laundryteria, until it shuttered its doors in 2020.

The *New Orleans City Directory* from 1952 lists a business at 901 Bourbon called the "Dunce Cap Bar, Bruno Robt owner."[10] City directories from previous years indicate that before that, it was the Bourbon Inn.[11] In the 1950s, the building had no gallery and no stucco; the exterior wood walls were painted yellow. The interior was remodeled for bar service, the two most notable renovations being the shape of the bar and the introduction of the eternal flame, both of which were designed like the bar at the old location to reflect the shape of the Mississippi River as it flows around the city. Sculptor Enrique Alferez, who had been a regular at Café Lafitte, designed both. In the early days, there was a liquor rack behind the bar in the same shape and a foot rail around the fountain; people could sit and place their drinks on the edge of the fountain, which sprayed water out of its three corners.

The story behind the eternal flame, like much of the bar's history—indeed, New Orleans itself—is shrouded in mystery and mythology. One common story claims the flame is a memorial to the original regular crowd's (and by extension, future generations of drinking gays') status as "exiles." Alferez never claimed that was what he had in mind when he gifted the artwork to the bar, but who knows? It makes for a nice story. In the early years, the flame also served as a fountain, but that function ceased when drunken barflies began using it as a urinal. A later owner of the bar declared the flame was a tribute to arson—arson that enabled him and his lover to buy Café Lafitte. The story goes that they set fire to their former business in another state and used the insurance money to buy Lafitte's.

Early photographs of the bar, dating from the mid-1950s, reveal a wooden structure with no gallery. Where the gallery now stands was a flimsy-looking awning with no support beams. The two side doors on Bourbon Street opposite the Clover Grill are closed and shuttered. On the frame of the main door

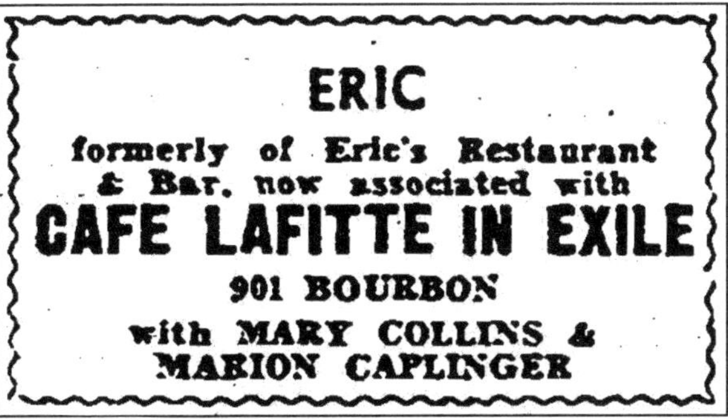

Ad in the *New Orleans Item*, 1957.

overlooking the intersection of Bourbon and Dumaine, in vertical letters, are the words CAFÉ LAFITTE IN EXILE. Next to the main door, facing Bourbon, are two small signs, which are illegible in the picture. To the left of the main door, on Dumaine, is another door. A photograph from 1962 suggests a paint job and the addition of a firebox on the corner of the intersection. The lettering of the sign is also changed, and window air-conditioning units have been added to the upstairs. The two small signs on the Bourbon Street facade are gone.

Over the decades, a myth has developed around the opening of the bar. Many of the stories concerning its reopening are predicated on the assumption that the bar was "in exile" because of its gay patrons, but as noted, that assumption may be erroneous. Some may ask why Caplinger and his partners didn't continue to lease the building at 941 Bourbon after the property was sold. There is some evidence that the new owner of the property did not want to cater to the old bar's queer clientele. It is possible the thought of losing such a significant percentage of his regular business played a factor in Caplinger's decision to relocate.

Some of the men we interviewed recall the grand opening of the new bar was celebrated with a costume party and that to avoid being discovered and raided, the front door was barricaded with sandbags and barbed wire. Those in the know had to enter through the back door. Still others maintain that on the night Café Lafitte in Exile opened, several gay regulars from the old location met there, had a few drinks, and then in unison stood up, picked up their barstools, and marched down the street to the new location. These accounts depict this action not only as an act of defiance but also as a rather dramatic coming out declaration. It's a nice story, but it sounds too good to be true.

GOING GAY

Hidden in these legends is an important question: just when did Café Lafitte in Exile become an exclusively gay bar? Circumstantial evidence and the testimony of gay men suggest that by 1958, the bar was predominantly gay. It is reasonable to assume, given Tom Caplinger's charisma and reputation and the new bar's physical proximity to the old one (one block), that most of his loyal customers, which included straight people, followed him to the new location. But did this loyalty survive Caplinger's death in 1956?

When Caplinger died in the bar (at 901 Bourbon) after closing time, sleeping on a cot, in March 1956, the *New Orleans Item* ran a front-page glowing article chronicling his contributions to the Vieux Carré, and every bar on Bourbon Street honored him by briefly dimming their lights and observing a moment of silence. The article includes reactions to his death from French Quarter luminaries such as Harnett Kane, who said, "I never knew a man who tried so hard to hide his kindness," and Ella Brennan, who commented: "He did more for the French Quarter than he ever got credit for. People will realize it more now that he's gone." And police officer John O'Rourke, who worked the Bourbon Street beat, said: "Let me tell you he was a type that'll never be duplicated. Bourbon St. owes a lot of its publicity to Tom. It was he who brought the writers around to all the spots to catch the entertainers."[12]

At the time of his death, Caplinger and his family were living across the street from Mother Cabrini's Day Home for Children. Shortly after he passed, one of the nuns knocked on his door and informed his widow that for the last ten years, Caplinger had been buying the milk for the children's lunches. Caplinger's wife, Marion, had no idea. After he died, Mary Collins would host séances to try to summon his spirit.

By the late 1950s, the bar was under the ownership of Tommy Hopkins, who lived in an upstairs apartment where the balcony bar now is. By all accounts, Hopkins, who was straight, was a thoroughly decent man who by all accounts harbored no prejudices against queer people and went out of his way to make the bar's gay clientele feel welcome. But he did not extend that same hospitality to Black people. These accounts beg a question—if Hopkins was not prejudiced against gay folk, why did he not allow Black people in the bar? It could be that Hopkins was not homophobic but was a racist, or it's possible he was not a racist but disallowed Black people in order to avoid police harassment.

Charlie, a friend of Hopkins and one of the few regulars from the 1950s still around, recalls the atmosphere of the bar: "It was a place where you could talk, where you could be yourself." He also recalls meeting Ernest Hemingway in the bar, "a total drunk who would talk your ear off, usually about politics."[13] Hemingway was not known to be gay, and his presence at the bar suggests it was still popular among straight people after its relocation. But by the end of the decade, the bar had earned a reputation as a gay bar.

Supporting this notion was the tragic murder of Fernando Rios in 1958 and the resulting sensational murder trial that followed the next year. In September 1958, three Tulane students—John S. Farrell, Alberto A. Calvo, and David P. Drennan—were arrested on murder charges. The three undergraduates had decided to go carousing in the French Quarter. At the beginning of their outing, Farrell suggested they "roll a queer"—a phrase that meant mugging a gay man. Calvo and Drennan initially dismissed the idea, but hours later, after a night of drinking, the two did not object when Farrell brought up the idea again. They chose Café Lafitte in Exile as their hunting ground. One wonders how they knew they could find a gay man at the bar.

Farrell entered Café Lafitte in Exile sometime after one thirty in the morning, while Calvo and Drennan waited outside. In the bar, Farrell met twenty-six-year-old Fernando Rios. The two men decided to "hook up" and left the bar together. Farrell and Rios entered an alley adjacent to St. Louis Cathedral, when Farrell began physically assaulting Rios. Calvo and Drennan, who were following behind, joined the attack. Rios, after being struck in the head several times and kicked repeatedly in the abdomen, died at Charity Hospital of a fractured skull about twelve hours after being discovered in the alley around 6:15 a.m.[14]

During a routine autopsy, the city coroner discovered the victim had an unusually thin cranium. Farrell, Calvo, and Drennan were arrested and charged with murder. The trial began on January 21, 1959. At trial, the defendants admitted to the beating but argued he died because of his "eggshell cranium," not because of their attack. Tortured logic aside, this defense made perfect sense to a homophobic, all-male, all-white jury in mid-twentieth-century New Orleans, and the three students were easily acquitted after the jury deliberated a mere two hours and fifteen minutes.

The acquittal and attendant press coverage of the trial provide a glimpse into the highly homophobic public attitudes toward "queers" at the time. When the "not guilty" verdict was announced, the courtroom erupted in applause and cheers for the jury. The *New Orleans States-Item* featured on its front page a picture of the defendants smiling broadly next to a boxed joke entitled "Today's Chuckle," which read, "Overheard in a night club: ordinarily I never chase a man, but this one was getting away."[15] The district attorney's office filed robbery charges against the three students, but that charge was reduced to theft, and the judge sentenced Farrell and Drennan to six months (Calvo had returned to his native Panama). The judge, George Platt, then immediately suspended the sentence. Throughout the ordeal, a deluge of letters poured into the editorial offices of the city's newspapers, the overwhelming majority of them supporting the gay-bashing murderers and calling on the city to "clean up the Quarter." The few letters in support of gays were often backhanded. One incensed reader argued that police should leave the gay bars alone so the "perverts" wouldn't feel compelled to mingle with "normal" people at straight bars. The fact that Farrell chose Café Lafitte in Exile as the place to find a gay target and the aforementioned letter both strongly suggest the bar was a well-known "queershop" by 1958.

Café Lafitte in Exile had well established itself as a gay cruise bar by the mid-1960s. This fact is established by a letter from the Armed Forces Disciplinary Control Board to the proprietor dated 1966:

> Dear Sir,
>
> As President of the Armed Forces Disciplinary Control Board serving this locality, it is my duty to inform you of certain undesirable conditions reported at your establishment which adversely affect the health and welfare of personnel in the Armed Forces.

Inspection reports presented to the Board indicate that your establishment is a known hangout for persons of undesirable character.

You are advised that it has become necessary for this Board, which I represent, to initiate action to have your establishment declared off-limits and out-of-bounds to personnel of the Armed Forces.

If you so desire, you may appear in person, with or without counsel, before this Board at its next meeting at 0930 hours, 14 July 1966, at the U.S. Coast Guard Station, Bayou St. John and Lakefront, New Orleans, Louisiana, to refute these allegations or to inform the Board of any remedial action you have taken, or contemplate, to correct the undesirable conditions.

It is requested that you inform the President of this Board if you plan to attend. Any questions relative to the foregoing may be addressed to the President, Armed Forces Disciplinary Control Board, U.S. Naval Air Station, New Orleans, Louisiana, and every effort will be made to clarify the matter for you.

Very truly yours,
W. F. Charles
Captain, U.S. Navy
President, AFDCB[16]

To this day, the letter is on proud and permanent framed display on the wall near the front door of the bar.

Sailors weren't the only people frequenting Lafitte's. By the late 1970s, the bar had earned a firmly entrenched reputation as the place to go to get laid. In his memoir, *1981—My Gay American Road Trip: A Slice of Our Pre-AIDS Culture,* JD Doyle describes Lafitte's as "a dark cruise bar."[17] In another travel memoir, Violet Quill cofounder Edmund White's classic, *States of Desire: Travels in Gay America,* quotes an Uptown man: "When I was seventeen . . . I started sneaking off to Lafitte's. I'd take her [his girlfriend] home after dates and usually end up at the bar. One night she was drunk and suspicious, and she followed me to the bar. At the bar she demanded that the bouncer let her in: 'I've come to see my husband.' She and I started having a knock-down drag-out when we suddenly looked up and there, coming down the stairs from the bar above, was her father!"[18]

Albert Carey told us he had heard of Lafitte's but said, "I was too chicken to go." We asked him if he remembered the first time he went to the bar. "Oh sure," he said. "I can give you the exact date: July 4, 1966—the day after I came out. I had spent the night with a really cute guy. The next day we went to the gay beach at Lake Pontchartrain and later to Lafitte's. I've been a regular ever since then."[19]

While the bar's patronage was predominantly gay at this time, it still attracted literary and artistic types. Carey describes Café Lafitte in Exile in those days as "a cocktail party to which you were always invited." Carey recalls meeting Truman Capote and Tennessee Williams there in the early 1970s:

> In those days I lived on Bourbon and frequented Lafitte's. One evening I saw Truman Capote sitting at the bar talking with someone. I approached him and said, "I don't mean to come on to you but I've always admired your work. May I buy you a drink?" And he responded, "Only if you sit and have one with us." He was so sweet, not at all bitchy like some have said. He even signed a beverage napkin for me. Another time I saw Tennessee Williams standing by the flame. As I neared him I could see he was very, very drunk but I introduced myself anyway. He gave me a very limp handshake, like a dead fish, and mumbled something incoherently, which kind of grossed me out, and he almost fell down in the process.[20]

Williams, whose last apartment in the French Quarter was a few blocks away, at 1014 Dumaine, was a regular at the bar until his death in 1983. John Meyers recalls meeting Williams at the bar in 1975:

> I was sitting at the bar, and I knew who he was, but I didn't make a big deal out of it. Then he came over and introduced himself as Tom, which was his given name. We fell into conversation, and he ended up taking me to lunch at Antoine's. I was in medical school at the time and thinking of going into psychiatry. He spoke of his sister's lobotomy—something I don't think he ever recovered from. He seemed more interested in drink-

ing than eating. In fact, I ate most of his food. We had a wonderful conversation and overall it was a delightful afternoon.[21]

A QUEER SUBCULTURE EMERGES

Because the 1950s were a decade of denial and invisibility for anyone who wasn't a straight, white, Christian male, a queer subculture began to emerge in those deeply closeted times that would eventually challenge the very notions of Ozzie and Harriet "normalcy" that defined the 1950s. Reminiscing on the gay scene in New Orleans in the 1950s, Café Lafitte in Exile regular Charlie summed up his feelings by saying the gay community was much more close-knit then because it had to be. Although a handful of gay bars were in competition, the bar owners communicated with each other and took a genuine interest in their clientele, often bailing them out of jail after raids or lending money to regulars who fell on hard times. There was a solidarity born of the oppressive climate that persisted well into the 1970s. When the police raided the Bourbon Pub and made several arrests, for example, owner Jerry Menefee bonded everyone out, had cabs waiting at the jail to return them to the bar, and then gave them free drinks for the rest of the night. Underage drinking in the 1950s was common and permitted primarily because the older gays knew all too well what it was like to be queer at sixteen or seventeen years old in a very straight world.[22] Of course, bailing your customers out of jail and providing an ample supply of young eye candy was good for business, but beyond that, there was a bona fide sense of camaraderie across the community—a sense that has diminished considerably in these out-and-proud times.

For much of the mid-twentieth century, gay life in New Orleans was centered in the Quarter in a few bars and in the homes of a few artists, writers, and photographers. In 1939, jazz musician "Miss Dixie" Fasnacht opened Dixie's Bar of Music in the Central Business District and in 1949 moved the bar to the Quarter. According to historian Roberts Batson, she may have been the model for a character in Gore Vidal's *The City and the Pillar* (1948). Although she retired in 1964, Miss Dixie, who died in 2011 at the age of 101, remains a legend, especially for her support of her patrons, who were frequently harassed by police during periodic "cleanup" campaigns. Hoyle Byrd remembers

Outside Dixie's Bar of Music on Mardi Gras, ca. 1950s. Richard R. Dixon / Cole Coleman Collection, gift of Mr. & Mrs. Richard R. Dixon, The Historic New Orleans Collection, acc. no. 1980.257.69.

the first time he went to Ms. Dixie's at the tender age of sixteen: "I was nervous, and Dixie must have seen it because she made me feel welcome and had me sit by the register, which was near the staircase, next to her sister who was the cashier. She told me if the place was raided, I could go upstairs and hide. She was the sweetest lady."[23]

For a brief time, there was also the Starlet Lounge and Tony Bacino's Bar. In addition to the bars in the Quarter, the famous Club My-O-My (featuring "female impersonators"), which flourished during the 1940s and 1950s, was located on the lakefront, and across town, on St. Claude, there was the Golden Feather, a bar that catered to African American gay men. There were also a few lesbian bars on Tchoupitoulas near the Irish Channel, but these were short-lived.[24] In the Quarter, Alice Brady opened Mascarade in 1952, the first of several lesbian bars she owned. Outside the bars, gay life manifested itself in private cocktail parties (one thinks of Dorian Greene's Peace Party soiree in John Kennedy Toole's *A Confederacy of Dunces*) and homes such as Lyle Saxon's literary salon on Royal Street and the home of famed lesbian photographer Francis Benjamin Johnston on Bourbon Street.

There were also unwritten rules and an understood protocol governing gay life in the 1950s and 1960s. More often than not, bartenders served as the arbiters and enforcers of this code of conduct. Sex workers, called "hustlers," for example, were relegated to a few bars in the upper Quarter, most notably Wanda's on Iberville and Mom's Society Page (where several bartenders were former priests) in Exchange Place Alley and had to operate under the watchful eyes of the bartenders. The same was true for johns. Rarely did hustler and john negotiate directly; rather, the bartender brokered such transactions, acting as advisor and referee to both parties.

Surreptitious codes were necessary for postwar queer America, especially in New Orleans, which was much more homophobic than recent generations can possibly imagine. Despite New Orleans's penchant for tolerance and its laissez-faire attitude, gays in New Orleans have historically faced a considerable amount of homophobia, especially from police. Although police harassment of queer bars now is mainly a thing of the past, it was, nonetheless, a very ugly past. Many bar owners, especially ones working with and for the Mafia, paid the police to leave them alone. The manager of a local restaurant recalls that when he was a regular at Café Lafitte in the 1960s, a police officer would come in each week like clockwork and collect an envelope stuffed with cash. Current Lafitte's owner Tom Wood stopped making the payments when he took over in the 1970s and eventually obtained a restraining order against the police because of their harassment.

Nevertheless, the vice squad would, on occasion, either raid bars or send undercover cops (almost always young and good-looking ones) into the bars to make arrests. This practice continued well into the 1970s. Albert Carey remembers meeting a good-looking young man at the bar who was an undercover police officer: "When he excused himself to go to the bathroom, the bartender told me to be careful because he was a vice cop."[25] Bartenders customarily slapped a wooden board on the bar to warn patrons they were getting too touchy-feely. Arrests were often accompanied by a police beating and pressure to name other "perverts." Anyone unfortunate enough to be arrested for "crimes against nature" or "committing a lewd act" often had their name and picture published in the *Times Picayune.* This could result in arrest, family alienation, loss of a job, eviction, and in some cases, commitment to a mental asylum. This type of harassment began to subside in the 1980s.

In 1955, police superintendent Provosty A. Dayries publicly proclaimed that homosexuals were the city's "Number One vice problem," adding, "They are the ones we want to get rid of most."[26] Widespread ignorance and familiar stereotypes of gay people were prevalent, especially the notion that homosexuals were predatory and looking to recruit teenagers and children. In 1951, the *Times-Picayune* ran a story entitled "Curb Advocated on Homosexuals: Crackdown to Save Young Persons Demanded":

> A warning that homosexuals in the French Quarter are at work corrupting high school boys and girls was made Friday by Richard R. Foster, chairman of the Mayor's Committee on the Vieux Carré, in an address before the Civic Council of New Orleans.
>
> For that reason, he said, the homosexual problem is one of the city's most serious. "In several instances, parents have come to police begging them to save their children," he asserted.
>
> High school boys and girls enticed into places habituated by homosexuals often see an obscene show or something of that nature as a starter," he added.

> The homosexuals are, he said, "continuously recruiting" and there are at least four "places" in the Quarter which cater to almost no one but homosexuals.
>
> "It almost seems as if youngsters who develop homosexual tendencies in other Southern cities are put on a train and sent to New Orleans," he said.[27]

About a month earlier, the *Times-Picayune* ran another article along the same lines but with a twist. At a meeting of the Mayor's Advisory Committee, Chairman Foster argued that the city should develop a strategy for discouraging so-called perverts from coming to New Orleans, claiming most homosexuals in New Orleans were "out-of-towners."[28] That gay people lived in New Orleans was either incomprehensible or too distasteful to bear. The level of denial and cluelessness revealed in the article illustrates the level of bigotry and hatred permeating straight society at the time. One man we interviewed noted, "We never flaunted our sexuality then because we were so afraid."[29]

Contributing to the homophobia of the time were deliberate actions by government authorities. In 1958, the city adopted a more pragmatic approach in its crusade to save the city from the "pink menace." In that year, the city council established a Committee on the Problem of Sex Deviates. An initial report of the committee proposed a "climate of hostility" be adopted toward homosexuals (as if the climate were not hostile enough). The committee's chairman was Jacob Morrison, a prominent citizen and cofounder of the Vieux Carré Property Owners and Associates. Morrison had been a thorn in the side of the gay community for years. He had, a few years earlier, led a successful effort to have the liquor license of the Starlet Lounge (at the corner of Chartres and St. Phillip) revoked, and Morrison then turned his attention to Tony Bacino's bar. In the summer of 1958, the manager and staff of Tony Bacino's were arrested six times. They were charged with violating this remarkable city ordinance: "No person of lewd, immoral, or dissolute character, sexual pervert . . . shall be employed" in bars and restaurants.[30] Amazingly, this ordinance was not repealed until 1993. After the last arrest, the manager and bartenders of Tony Bacino's filed for, and were awarded, an injunction and temporary restraining order. They subsequently filed a lawsuit but lost the case on appeal.

Public attitudes of the 1950s changed little in the 1960s. Because gays were forced to live in the closet, cracking the closet door open for a few hours at a gay bar was a particularly intense experience, both relieving but also awkward, not to mention dangerous, which added a titillating element to cruising. Having been denied both the means and opportunity to develop an open system of courtship, those precious few hours at the gay bar were usually spent cutting to the chase, which is to say sucking and fucking without the arduous process of ritualized courtship.

A PLACE TO GET LAID

In the 1960s, years before the sexual revolution and, later, the AIDS crisis, Café Lafitte in Exile saw a lot of action. One old-timer, Ron, recalls that "all you had to do to get laid at Café Lafitte was show up."[31] Ron, who was quick to point out in his interview that he never "worked" the pool table (or roadside toilets for that matter), remembers one memorable weekend when he commandeered the restroom upstairs and serviced multiple men. Rumor has it that Confederate president Jefferson Davis's great-grandson used to hang out in the bar and give free blow jobs in the bathroom in the late 1960s.

Ralph, a fifty-year veteran of Lafitte's, remembers first coming to the bar in 1964, at the tender age of nineteen. Initially, the bouncer wouldn't let him in because he looked too young. Ralph produced a driver's license, but the bouncer wouldn't budge. Incensed, Ralph stormed off in search of a police officer to validate the license. After explaining his dilemma, the officer asked Ralph if he knew what kind of bar Lafitte's was. Ralph said yes, and the cop shrugged his shoulders, walked him back to the bar, and told the bouncer to let him in.[32]

At first, Ralph was struck by how "classy" the bar was, especially when compared to the few gay bars he had been to in Memphis. For the next few years, Ralph would come to New Orleans from Tennessee three or four times a year, until he finally moved to the Quarter. He describes Lafitte's in the late 1960s and '70s as having "a marvelous mix of people" and observes the bar's "attention to detail" is what made it distinctive. As an example, Ralph remembers with fondness the juicing machine, which enabled bar patrons to witness firsthand their cocktails mixed with freshly squeezed juice. And the upstairs, he recalls, was redecorated every few years.

Mardi Gras 1969 was a special one for Ralph. He had come down from Memphis with a hundred dollars (beer was sixty-five cents then). He met Billy, who had been a student at Tulane, by the eternal flame, and the two fell madly in love. They moved briefly to California and eventually broke up after a year together. The experience transformed Ralph's life and helped him nudge his closet door more open than it had ever been before. Ralph remembers Billy, who was a bit older, telling him stories of meeting and drinking with Tennessee Williams, Truman Capote, and Gore Vidal at Lafitte's.

Since the French Quarter had so many gay bars, a lot of young men in the closet in small towns or rural areas flocked to New Orleans. In 1965, John Tinsley was an undergraduate at Louisiana State University in Baton Rouge. During his sophomore year, he came out of the closet and moved off campus into a rental house with his gay friends. One day, a straight friend saw him hanging out with an obviously gay young man and promptly reported this disturbing news to the dean of men. John was called into the dean's office and gravely informed the university had compiled a dossier on him, specifically detailing his association with sexual deviates. He was also told he needed to move back onto campus. "You need to get away from those people," the dean informed him, adding: "If you move back on campus, this file goes away. If you don't, I'll tell your parents you're hanging around with queers." Tinsley recalls considering suicide: "I almost jumped off the top of Tiger Stadium. I lost all my straight friends, and my gay friends wanted nothing to do with me. I had become a pariah. Shortly after the episode, a straight friend from back home in Shreveport invited me to go to Mardi Gras in New Orleans. Once there, I managed to slip away from my straight friend and head to the gay bars. At Diogynes, I met Tommy. I ended up staying the entire weekend with him. We dated for a year and a half."[33]

The upstairs bar at Lafitte's, especially the pool table area, has always been fertile ground for anonymous trysts and spontaneous encounters. Rip Naquin-Delain, founder and publisher of *Ambush Magazine,* recalls going to Lafitte's in the late 1970s. It was the Friday before Mardi Gras, and he was in town to attend a Mardi Gras ball. Afterward, he and some friends went to Lafitte's. As they ascended the stairs, Rip remembers being shocked at the scene: "Everyone was naked and having sex and here we were in our tuxes. We were lucky to get out with our clothes on."[34]

GAY CARNIVAL

Like the bars, the Gay Carnival krewes also afforded the community a semi-safe space to socialize as well as an outlet for its creative and artistic talents. In 1949, Bob Demmons founded the Lundi Gras Luncheon, the oldest continuing non-bar-related activity in the New Orleans gay community. A few years later, in 1953, the Steamboat Club, the oldest gay social organization in New Orleans, was founded. For a time, the Steamboat Club met upstairs at Café Lafitte, when it housed the short-lived restaurant the Streetcar.

The first Gay Carnival club, the Krewe of Yuga (KY), was founded by Doug Jones in 1958, in part as a way to spoof the seriousness with which the traditional, old-line krewes took themselves. This satirical genesis echoes the founding of the Zulu Social Aid and Pleasure Club fifty years earlier, which began as a spoof of Rex, the King of Carnival. Yuga flourished until the police raided its 1962 ball, which was held in Metairie. The 1962 ball was off to a good start. The costumes were fabulous, alcohol was flowing, and aging French Quarter legend Elmo Avet, who owned an antique store on Royal Street—and that day was dressed as Mary, Queen of Scots—awaited being crowned Yuga Regina V. But it was not to be. Before the tableau began, Jefferson Parish police arrived at the Rambler Room, kicked open the doors, and raided the ball. Pandemonium ensued, and many fled the building by jumping out of windows. Several ran into the adjacent woods but were stopped when the police dogs approached. Nearly one hundred men were arrested.

Those who escaped arrest eventually made it back to the safety of the French Quarter. Miss Dixie, upon being alerted of the raid, dispatched her attorney with a wad of cash from her bar safe to bail everyone out of jail. The morning following the raid, Elmo Avet and Bill Woolley, both of whom had avoided arrest, sat at the Bourbon House across from Dixie's and debriefed the previous evening's fiasco.

So, who tipped off the police? It's easy to assume that naturally the conservative, suburbanite housewives of Metairie in 1962 had called the police when they saw a bunch of men dressed in drag entering their local day care facility, but a much more tantalizing theory involves a jilted drag queen. Hell hath no fury . . .

Candy Lee hailed from Cajun country and found her way to New Orleans, where she secured work as a "female impersonator" at the legendary Club My-O-My. She also worked as a bartender at Tony Bacino's, which in 1958 was raided several times by the police. Candy Lee was arrested repeatedly.[35]

Convinced the raids were the result of a tip to the police from a fellow queen who had a proverbial axe to grind with her, Candy Lee, never one to be soft-spoken, loudly and repeatedly told several people who she thought had snitched on Tony Bacino's. Her accusation was never verified, and it may not have been true at all since the mayor's Committee on the Problem of Sex Deviates, created to rid the French Quarter of homosexuals, harassed several queershops.

Candy Lee raised so much hell about the raids that by the early 1960s, she had been banned from the two gay krewes that existed at the time—Yuga and Petronius—and was generally considered a persona non grata.

In the aftermath of the 1962 Yuga raid, many speculated, among them Yuga founder Doug Jones, that Candy Lee had tipped off the police that a wild stag party involving cross-dressing homosexuals was occurring at the Rambler Room dance studio, thus exacting her revenge.

Fearing arrest and the subsequent public outing that accompanied such raids, several men ran out of the building and hid in the nearby woods. Of the mayhem, gay carnival historian Albert Cary writes: "One story has the Queen hiding in these bushes as the troopers came through with their flashlights. Sparkling in the high beams of light, his rhinestone tiara gave him away."[36] After the raid, Miss Dixie hired an attorney for those arrested and paid many of the jailed men's bail. The next day's paper published the names of nearly one hundred men arrested in the raid. The krewe folded as a result of the ensuing scandal, but from the ashes of Yuga arose several other gay krewes.

One of the names in the paper the day after the raid was Carlos Rodriguez, the first Queen of Petronius. Petronius was founded in 1961 and held its first ball in 1962. Two founding members of Petronius—Bill Woolley and Elmo Avet—had also been at the ill-fated Yuga Ball but managed to elude the police. Under their leadership, Petronius obtained a state charter and became an incorporated Carnival krewe.

Candy Lee became something of a legend when she inspired Tennessee Williams's *And Tell Sad Stories of the Death of Queens.* Lee and Williams had become friends, and the playwright was fascinated by her life story. Lee often regaled Williams with the various tales of woe that constituted her life at bars in the Quarter and at her apartment on Decatur Street. Lee and Williams and Jones and Dixie and Yuga are long gone now, but Gay Carnival survives. Various members of Yuga would go to found other krewes, including Petronius, Amon Ra, Armeinius, Ganymede, and Celestial Knights. In their heyday, before the AIDS crisis, there were close to twenty Gay Carnival krewes (including one lesbian krewe, Ishtar).

Reminiscing on the early Yuga balls, member John Bogie recalled: "The Yuga Regina was one of the most spectacular sights I've ever seen in my life. When the lights reflected off her royal raiments, the room was filled with explosions and bursts of light like fireworks. Who would have guessed that her children would take up the mantle of Carnival and run with it like they were possessed?"[37]

In the 1960s, as queer communities in California, Chicago, and New York began to organize politically, the gay community in New Orleans was much more enthusiastic about organizing socially, as exemplified in the growth of Gay Carnival. More than a few observers have noted that "Mardi Gras is kind of gay." Edmund White offers valuable insights on this phenomenon in his landmark book from 1980, *States of Desire:*

> Mardi Gras is largely a gay holiday and drag contests are a central part of the festivities . . . I chatted with a young man from an old Cajun family who told me that he belongs not to one of the official Krewes but to an informal circle of actors, writers and painters who give eight costume balls during the season . . . In this man's opinion, gay activism in New Orleans is social, not political. "Many prominent New Orleanians, even those who are married, are gay and they are eager to protect gays. Gay life is well integrated into the life of the city."[38]

The Catholic Church claims Shrove Tuesday as a religious holiday, one last chance to party before Ash Wednesday and the Lenten season, but Carnival's pagan roots stretch back to the time before Christ was born, and New Orleans knows full well it doesn't need a reason to party, much less a sanctimonious one. No, Carnival stems from the deepest core of what New Orleans is—a pagan-Baroque fantasy realm realized, a magical make-believe playground, a mythical place of transformation.

Carnival in New Orleans is in many ways a reincarnation of the tableaux of King Louis XIV's Royal Court, a court whose debauchery, according to historians Will and Ariel Durant, rivaled pagan Rome at its most depraved. Consider the names of the most popular Mardi Gras krewes: Comus (God of Revelry and Excess), Momus (God of Satire), Bacchus (God of Wine), Proteus (God of the Sea and Mutability), Orpheus (God of Poets and Musicians), Endymion (God of Shepherds and Hunters), and Rex (the King of Carnival). These krewes are essentially private social clubs, and it is they who annually host elaborate Carnival balls and produce the parades for which Mardi Gras is so well-known. The oldest is the Mistick Krewe of Comus, founded in 1856. The name derives from Milton's masque "Comus." All the folkloric value of Mardi Gras is lost on those who view it as merely a massive drunken street orgy. S. Frederick Starr argues correctly the vulgarity of Mardi Gras is superficial, that in substance, Mardi Gras is "a poetic festival steeped in the exquisite high art of allegory."[39]

Consider the highly ritualized hallmarks of "official" Mardi Gras: by noon, Rex, King of Carnival, has arrived at Gallier Hall. The parade stops so the mayor can toast Rex. After a short speech, in which the mayor decrees that merriment and revelry shall rule the day, he lifts a glass of champagne and declares, "Hail Rex!" The massive crowd follows suit, each person raising his or her drink simultaneously, exclaiming, "Hail Rex!" as Rex waves his scepter over the crowd and commands his subjects to have fun. At 11:30 p.m., the Rex Carnival Ball comes to a halt as Rex, his Queen, and the rest of his royal court make their way to pay their respects to Comus and his court at the Comus Carnival Ball. This meeting of the courts is the ritual highlight of the Carnival season. The courts meet, toasts are made, and the band strikes up "If Ever I Cease to Love," which heralds the end of Carnival. At 12:00 a.m., Ash Wednesday is welcomed by seven policemen on horseback in wedge formation, beginning the ritual sweep of Bourbon Street. Starting at Canal and followed by a small army of state troopers, they make their way down the infamous neon strip. The leader, armed with a bullhorn, bellows to the boozing hordes: "Mardi Gras is now over. It is Ash Wednesday. Ashes are now available at St. Louis Cathedral."

Much like New Orleans itself, Mardi Gras is a wonderfully complex cultural phenomenon, replete with layers and layers of meaning and symbolism. It is revelry, pageantry and fantasy—who better to embody it than the gay community?

Drag performances have been associated with Mardi Gras in New Orleans since the early years of the city's existence. The earliest written reference to Mardi Gras dates back to 1729. In that year, Marc-Antoine Caillot, a bureaucrat working for the Louisiana office of the Company of the Indies, wrote in his journal:

> The next day, which was Lundi Gras, I went to the office where I found my companions who were bored to death. I proposed to them that we form a party of revelers and go to Bayou Saint John . . . As for myself, I was dressed as a shepherdess in white. I had a corset of white dimity, a muslin skirt, a large pannier . . . along with plenty of beauty marks too. I had my husband, who was the Marquis of Carnival; he had a suit trimmed with gold braid on all the seams . . . What also made it hard for people to recognize me was that I had shaved very closely that evening and had a number of beauty marks on my face, and even on my breasts, which I had plumped up. I was also the one out of all my group who was dressed up the most coquettishly . . . Unless you looked at me very closely, you could not tell that I was a boy.[40]

Hoyle Byrd, who reigned as the thirtieth Queen of Petronius, thirty-fifth King of Petronius, and the fifth Queen of Satyricon, remembers a Carnival highlight from 1969: "Our Krewe Captain had a beautiful apartment at the corner of St. Peter and Royal. In those days the parades still rolled through the Quarter down Royal Street. So there we were on the balcony in our elaborate costumes, part of which were hanging over the balcony, when Comus noticed us. He stopped his parade and then toasted us. That was special."[41]

By the early 1970s, meeting space became an issue for the growing number of gay krewes. Many locations were already reserved for the main-line nongay krewes. Other locations could no longer accommodate the crowds that gay balls were attracting or chose to turn a cold shoulder to them in light of the increasing visibility of the national gay rights movement. A few krewes held their balls in Black union labor halls. The civic center in neighboring Chalmette became home to several krewes, which is odd because one doesn't normally associate St. Bernard Parish with tolerance and diversity.

In 1976, a disgruntled Bill Woolley broke away from Petronius and founded Celestial Knights. At its first ball, Celestial Knights tried to outshine Petronius. But Petronius, the grande dame of Gay Carnival, would not be upstaged. In an article celebrating Petronius's fiftieth anniversary, Howard Smith writes: "But the Queen of Petronius would not be outshone by her children. In her 'Fantasie de la Mer' ball, the queen's costume at the end of the ball revealed her in a gloriously sequined octopus gown with tentacles spreading out to cover the entire stage. She had, for the moment, retained her luster."[42]

Woolley was not the first, nor the last, member of a krewe to grow dissatisfied and break away to form another krewe. In 2000, longtime Petronius captain Mickey Gil and sixteen others left to form the Mistick Krewe of Satyricon. Gil had joined Petronius in 1985, just as many krewes folded because their ranks had been decimated by the AIDS epidemic. Many credit Gil with reviving Petronius, and by extension, gay carnival, in that dark period. When he died, in 2010, an article in the *Times-Picayune* honored his legacy.

Currently, there are several active gay carnival krewes: Amon-Ra, Apollo, Armeinius, Lords of Leather, Mwindo, Narcissus, Petronius, and Rue Royale Revelers. In addition to the gay krewes, another immensely popular feature of gay Mardi Gras is the Bourbon Street Awards. From 1974 to 1985, Café Lafitte in Exile sponsored the event. In later years, the contest was held at the corner of Bourbon and St. Ann and more recently at the corner of St. Ann and Dauphine. Favored by drag queens and characterized by elaborate costumes (many of which premiered at the Carnival balls a few weeks earlier), the contest draws the annual attention of the international media.

Local independent filmmaker Tim Wolff has chronicled the history of gay Mardi Gras in a documentary entitled *The Sons of Tennessee Williams,* which premiered on the New Orleans public broadcasting station WYES in 2011. In the film, Wolff argues the gay krewes constituted a form of gay political activism. This claim requires some qualification. The gay krewes were essentially social in nature and were not formed to further a political agenda like, say, the Human Rights Campaign or the Forum for Equality later would. Nevertheless, many members of the krewes were prominent members of straight New Orleans society and business circles. And some of these men did engage in activism (those who organized the Anita Bryant protests, for example, were members of gay krewes), but they did not do so under the auspices of their krewe names. Also, it is important to remember that in the 1960s, gay men were routinely denied the right to free assembly (except perhaps at bars, but even that was a dicey situation given the alarming frequency and terrible consequences of police raids). The Krewe of Petronius obtaining a state charter was, therefore, a political act but not in the traditional sense of gay activism as we think of the term today.[43]

The early 1970s were a time of great change not only for Café Lafitte in Exile but also for the community in general. The physical appearance of Café Lafitte in Exile had remained unchanged for nearly twenty years until it underwent a major facelift in 1972. A few years earlier, in 1969, Laisder Mendoza, the twenty-five-year-old son of a Venezuelan industrialist, had a heated argument with his lover in the bar and was asked by the staff to leave. Enraged, Mendoza stormed out of the bar, got into his pickup truck, which was parked across the street, and drove it through the front door of the bar. Three patrons were slightly injured, and two were taken to Charity Hospital, while the third fled the scene before the police arrived, presumably for fear of being outed. Twenty feet of the Bourbon Street facade was ripped away. Albert Carey, a regular who lived a block away, remembers the day after the incident: "The crash occurred on a Friday, but the next night was business as usual, minus the wall, of course." With the insurance money—and the assistance of gay architect Leon Impastato—Tommy Hopkins, who now owned the bar, covered the wood structure with stucco and added the balcony.

In those days, the ceiling was covered with business cards, and the walls of the bar were always covered with paintings by local artists. Eventually, all these pieces sold, with the exception of one—a portrait of a woman baring her breast. This painting became a fixture of the bar and came to be known by regulars as "Mother." In 1975, when Hopkins sold the bar, he refused to part with the work and had a copy of it made. It still hangs in the bar today.

Café Lafitte in Exile in 2010. Collins C. Diboll Vieux Carré Digital Survey, The Historic New Orleans Collection, 2_076_bour_901_a.

POLITICAL ACTIVISM

At the dawn of the 1970s, as the seeds of political activism were planted in New Orleans and blossoming in other cities, two events served to stifle the burgeoning optimism: the sensational trial of Clay Shaw and the tragic arson at the Up Stairs Lounge. Shaw's trial served as a warning to gay men they better stay in the closet—a notion reinforced by the public reaction to the tragic Up Stairs Lounge arson. And while all this was happening, a small group of friends hosted a house party that would grow into one of the largest annual celebrations of queerness in the world.

All the gay bars suffered a bit in the late 1960s because of District Attorney Jim Garrison's prosecution of well-known businessman Clay Shaw, one of many notable characters to have frequented Café Lafitte in Exile. Shaw had achieved notoriety by being the only person ever tried in the John F. Kennedy assassination, and even though he was ultimately acquitted, his memory was further defamed by Oliver Stone's depiction of him in the film *JFK.* The trial and the movie have overshadowed Shaw's true legacy: that of a war hero, a civic leader, a French Quarter preservationist, and a successful playwright. Prior to the Garrison trial, Shaw, like countless other closeted gay leaders, was revered and respected. In 1965, the city of New Orleans awarded him its highest honor, the International Order of Merit. Many in New Orleans resent not only Stone's negative depiction of Shaw but also Jim Garrison's persecution of him. One man we interviewed, Louis, summed up the feelings of many when he called Garrison "a piece of shit who ruined Shaw."[44]

One man who knew Shaw was Otis Fennel, former owner of Faubourg Marigny Arts and Books—the first gay and feminist-themed bookstore in the South. When Oliver Stone was researching *JFK,* he hired Otis as consultant for the scenes that dealt with Clay Shaw. Shaw frequented Lafitte's so as part of the field research for the movie, Otis brought Stone to the bar. Stone told him it was the first gay bar he had ever been to. According to Otis, Stone disregarded most of the material he provided and then refused to pay him for his consulting work. So there.

Garrison's pursuit of Shaw has been the source of much speculation. It's an open secret that Garrison was a closet case or at least bisexual. One politically connected patron of Lafitte's is convinced that Garrison went after Shaw because both men were chasing the same twink. (It is generally conceded that Shaw had a fondness for "chicken"; several old-timers recalled that seeing Shaw cruising the Quarter in his convertible filled with young men was a common sight.) A local monsignor who socialized with Shaw regularly is also implicated in this theory, but our source declined to elaborate on the good father's involvement. Another source of Garrison's persecution of Shaw may have been an incident one evening at Brennan's. According to legend, Garrison was at the famed restaurant dining with his first wife when the two got into a heated argument. At some point, Garrison became so enraged, he slapped his wife. Shaw, who was seated at a table nearby, came over and told Garrison: "Jim, cut it out. You're not at Tony Bacino's." Garrison responded bitterly, threatening Shaw, "I'll get you for that."[45]

Yet another theory about Garrison's motivation suggests the Shaw trial was an elaborate diversionary tactic to draw attention away from a brewing personal scandal that threatened to destroy Garrison. In 1969, a grand jury investigated allegations that Garrison had molested a thirteen-year-old boy at the New Orleans Athletic Club. At the urging of Archbishop Philip Hannan, and perhaps out of privacy concerns for the victim, the boy's family eventually dropped the charges, but the grand jury foreman, William J. Krummel, confirmed to columnist Jack Anderson the grand jury had indeed looked into the allegations. Krummel never made a public comment about the investigation because he feared retribution by the District Attorney's Office.

In 1998, Patricia Lambert published *False Witness: The Real Story of Jim Garrison's Investigation and Oliver Stone's film JFK.* In her research for the book, Lambert interviewed the victim and his family about the incident as well as others who knew Garrison. The portrait that emerges is not at all flattering. David Chandler, a journalist and personal friend of Garrison, described Garrison as "basically a pedophile."[46] And Rosemary James, one of the reporters who broke the news of Garrison's investigation of Shaw, notes Garrison "used to slap his wife around in public all the time."[47] James Kirkwood, who won a Pulitzer Prize and a Tony Award for writing *A Chorus Line,* was a personal friend of Shaw's and also wrote a book about the trial, *American Grotesque.* In 2021, Louisiana State University history professor Alecia Long published *Cruising for Conspirators: How a New Orleans DA Prosecuted the Kennedy Assassination as a Sex Crime.*

Historian Roberts Batson has argued that Garrison's prosecution of Shaw adversely affected the psyche of gay New Orleans. In his column in *Impact,* Batson described Mayor Maurice "Moon" Landrieu's appointment of Clay Shaw to the French Market Corporation as an act of redemption for Shaw. Batson says the appointment was "arguably the most significant political act for gay people in the entire decade."[48]

Other men we interviewed also recall seeing Garrison in various gay bars from time to time, particularly Le Round Up. It should be noted that Garrison was originally assigned to the prosecution team that tried the three Tulane students accused of murdering Fernando Rios in 1958. For reasons that have never been clarified, he was replaced with another assistant district attorney.

Shaw's trial dovetailed with the modern gay rights movement, which was just coming into its own at the time. Many gay men of the time believed that

Clay Shaw, 1972. C. F. Weber Collection, Williams Research Center, The Historic New Orleans Collection, acc. no. 2012.0208.2.111.

District Attorney Garrison's pursuit of Shaw was motivated by internalized homophobia. Consequently, they were reluctant to organize politically. That's not to say there wasn't any gay activism in New Orleans, but in retrospect, it's fair to say the persecution of Clay Shaw helped stifle locally the gay political activism burgeoning elsewhere in the nation as a result of Stonewall. There were, however, a few efforts at organizing in the early 1970s.

Despite the budding gay liberation movement that was gaining momentum on both coasts, gay men and women in New Orleans still feared being outed. Paul, a regular at Lafitte's for over forty years, recalls the fear of police the first time he went to the bar in the early 1970s. At that time, police raids were still common, and whenever a stranger entered the bar, everyone tensed up and usually fell silent. A friendly pat on the back was considered by authorities sufficient grounds for arrest. No one knew Paul at the time, so Jerry Menefee, the bartender, asked him if he was a vice cop.

"No," Paul replied.
"Then why are you here?"
"This is a gay bar, right?
"Maybe."
"Well, I'm here to get laid."

Jerry then grabbed a handful of napkins, tossed them in the air, and announced loudly: "It's okay boys. He's one of us."[49] Paul went on to get laid several times that night. Paul lived in Houma, an hour and half away from New Orleans, but would drive in on the weekends. On one of these trips, Paul met his lover, upstairs at the Bourbon Pub. They were together thirty years, until Paul died.

In addition to police harassment, there was also plenty of freelance homophobia in the 1970s. Paul recalls a couple of "rednecks" were walking down Bourbon Street when they noticed a drag queen sitting at the bar inside Lafitte's. One of them stuck his head in the door and yelled, "Faggots!" The drag queen they noticed was the notorious Daisy Mae, who worked security at the bar. Enraged, Daisy Mae proceeded to "kick their asses," according to Paul. After the drubbing, Daisy Mae stuck one of her very high heels on the redneck's throat and proudly proclaimed, "You just got your ass whooped by a faggot!"[50]

John Meyers, local doctor who was also one of the first bartenders at the Bourbon Pub, recalls that each time he and his friends left Café Lafitte, they would look up and down Bourbon and Dumaine Streets to check not only for police but also for anyone who might recognize them.

Sometimes police raided bars at the request of concerned citizens. One retired police officer remembers an incident from the early 1970s. A man notified the police that his sixteen-year-old son had run away from home and that he had tracked him to New Orleans. The father had located his son and followed him to a gay bar in the Quarter; now he was asking the police to retrieve him. As the police entered the bar and proceeded upstairs, they were puzzled by two large cans of Crisco at the top of the stairs. Then they beheld a sight they had surely never imagined before. There, on the pool table, the young lad was lying on his back, legs high in the air, next to another teenager (both au naturel), while a throng of eager patrons stood in line, dollops of Crisco in hand.

Frustration with police harassment had sparked Stonewall, widely—and erroneously—regarded to be the birth of the modern gay rights movement. The reaction to Stonewall and the movement it symbolized is impossible to separate from the milieu in which it occurred: the sexual revolution, the civil rights movement, women's liberation, protests against the Vietnam War, the destabilization of white, Christian hegemony. People from every group who had been discriminated against and oppressed were rising out of their apathy and agitating for their rights, and queer folk were no exception. In New Orleans, however, the gay community was slow to organize politically and remained generally lackadaisical in demanding equality.

It was at this time that a few brave politicians began to view the gay community as a potential voting bloc. Longtime district attorney Harry Connick Sr. was the first candidate to court the gay vote in his first unsuccessful run for the office in 1969. Meeting with several members of the gay community, Connick promised to end the long-standing practice of police raids of gay bars. At the meeting, which was mostly a question-and-answer session, a notoriously outspoken drag queen named Jo Jo Landry dared to ask the question that was on everyone's mind: "Let's cut the crap. What we really want to know is, are we going to go to jail if we get caught sucking dick in the bars?"[51] Connick answered yes, noting that public sex acts were illegal regardless of who performed them. Connick lost the 1969 election but did manage to unseat Jim Garrison in 1973. And despite his overtures to the gay community, he was still not above pandering to a homophobic public. He made headlines in 1977 when he announced "the net is closing in" on sixteen men suspected of operating a "homosexual ring" out of a local Boy Scout troop.[52] The public perception of gay men as pedophiles was consistently reinforced in the media. For instance, a year earlier, seventy men were arrested in City Park and

Audubon Park during a one-month period in the summer of 1976 on charges of obscenity or crimes against nature.[53]

The Gay Liberation Front (GLF) of New Orleans was founded in 1970 by Lynn Miller and David Solomon. Although the group fell apart by mid-1971, in that brief span, it had produced the first gay public action, a demonstration of about seventy-five people at City Hall protesting police harassment. The march on City Hall received moderate coverage in the press. The *Times-Picayune* even printed the marchers' demands:

1. An immediate end of all hostility, brutality, entrapment and harassment by the New Orleans Police of gay men and women and of their places of gathering.
2. Formation of a Governor's Panel empowered to conduct a complete and thorough investigation of the police methods and actions against gay people. On this panel shall sit one gay man and one gay woman.
3. The immediate suspension from duty of Police Superintendent Clarence Giarusso and Vice Squad head Souler, until the Governor's Panel has completed its investigation. Should the panel find against these men, they shall be terminated immediately.[54]

City officials ignored the protest publicly, but behind the scenes, Richard Kernion, a mayoral assistant, facilitated a meeting between GLF leaders and the New Orleans police chief. Journalist Robert Fieseler writes: "A genuine cessation of hostilities followed, and the mayor's office made a statement that no newspapers chose to print: 'Superintendent Giarusso stated that no citizens would be harassed in any way provided that they were not molesting others or otherwise breaking the law.'"[55] The truce lasted for about three years.

The GLF's demands did not go unnoticed. Straight New Orleans was shocked not only at the visibility of gay people but also, perhaps more so, at the alarming fact they were demanding things. While the Gay Liberation Front disturbed many straight people, it also gave hope to many gays who were still in the closet. One man we interviewed told us it had never occurred to him to live openly gay until the GLF's march on City Hall.

The GLF also published the first gay-identified publication; a newsletter entitled *Sunflower.* The first edition featured testimonials from several men, one of whom was straight, who were harassed, beaten, and arrested while in or near Cabrini Park, which was, apparently, quite the cruising ground. The GLF also presented the first Stonewall commemoration, a June 1971 "Gay-In" in City Park. Out of the organizing efforts of the Gay Liberation Front, individuals soon founded a Metropolitan Community Church congregation, a Daughters of Bilitis chapter, and a gay student organization at Tulane University.[56]

Dovetailing with the emerging women's liberation movement, lesbians began to organize, and several women's groups were formed, including a lesbian music festival. Many lesbians became involved with the National Organization for Women (NOW) in an effort to get the Equal Rights Amendment (ERA) passed. A Lesbian Task Force was formed and even traveled around the state on educational tours. Clay Latimer, an early lesbian activist who was arrested in a raid at the lesbian bar Charlene's, remembers bringing a typewriter and index cards to Charlene's to solicit political messages from patrons. "Charlene's didn't mind political activity, but that sort of thing was forbidden at Alice Brady's bars."[57]

The Up Stairs Lounge fire also produced a spurt of activism, but these efforts were short-lived. On June 24, 1973, a Sunday evening, an unruly sex worker, Roger Dale Nunez, was physically thrown out of the Up Stairs Lounge bar for badgering and fighting with a regular customer, Mike Scarborough. Scarborough was in the bathroom when Nunez, who was in the next stall, started harassing him through the glory hole. Scarborough complained to the bartender. As Nunez was being escorted out the bar, he threatened to "burn you all out." About thirty minutes later, a fire broke out on the stairwell. As the fire spread, panic ensued. Bartender Buddy Rasmussen led about twenty people through a rear fire exit, which was not clearly marked. Many dashed for the windows, but they had iron bars to prevent intoxicated patrons from falling out. A few men, including a man named Rusty, were skinny enough to squeeze through and drop to safety, but the others were doomed.

Katherine Kirsch was on her way to buy cigarettes around 7:45 p.m., when she smelled smoke at the corner of Iberville and Chartres. She opened the stairwell, saw the flames, and immediately ran to the Midship Bar next door to call the police. Fire trucks arrived about two minutes later. They were met by a grizzly, horrific scene. A few people who had jumped lay charred on the sidewalk. The lifeless body of Bill Larson, pastor of the local Metropolitan Community Church, was wedged in the window, his face and right arm protruding stiffly over the street. Buddy Rasmussen saw his boyfriend, Adam Fontenot, knocked off his feet with a blast from a fire hose while he flayed around on fire. George Mitchell had escaped the fire but ran back in to rescue his boyfriend, Louis Broussard; both died. Many of the dead were burned beyond recognition but were ultimately identified through the records of local dentist Perry Waters, who also perished in the fire.

Twenty-nine people died that night, three more in the days that followed. Nunez died by suicide the following year. According to drag queen Marcy Marcel and several others, Nunez killed himself because he was so full of remorse. Although Marcel was a regular at the Up Stairs Lounge on Sunday nights at the time, she had stayed home that night to watch a Bette Davis movie that was airing on television.

Initial media reports and the police response to the fire were less than sympathetic. Some family members of the deceased refused to claim the ashes of their "loved" ones. Radio commentators joked the remains should be buried in fruit jars. Church after church refused the use of their facilities for a memorial service. The Unitarian church hosted a small service, and Father Bill Richardson of St. George's Episcopal Church believed the dead, despite their lifestyles, should have a service and graciously allowed, over the protest of many parishioners, the use of St. George's sanctuary. Marcy Marcel, who was at the service, echoed the feelings of others when she recalled being relieved to see her friends alive, if not altogether well, at the service. A larger service was then held at St. Mark's United Methodist Church on the edge of the French Quarter.

The Up Stairs Lounge arson attracted gay activists from all over the country to New Orleans, most notably Reverend Troy Perry, founder of the Metropolitan Community Church. Perry and others chastised the gay community of New Orleans for its apathetic attitude and general lethargy regarding the gay liberation movement so much in vogue in other American cities at the time. Local bar owners and prominent gay men responded by calling Perry and the other activists "carpetbaggers" and "outside agitators." John Meyers, a retired obstetrician who had worked his way through medical school by bartending at several gay bars, recalls meeting Perry at Café Lafitte and telling him firmly, "Leave us alone." Looking back thirty-eight years later, Meyers admitted, "Perry was right."[58]

The fire motivated a handful of activists to form the Gay People's Coalition (GPC). The GPC launched another publication, *Causeway,* and established the "Gay Crisis Phone Line." *Causeway* was edited anonymously by a student at Tulane named Bill Rushton, who also edited the *Vieux Carré Courier.*[59] An editorial from the January 1974 edition of *Causeway* declared, "There are enough gay men and women in N.O. who are able to do anything they wish—be it swinging an election or electing a gay city councilman."[60] This clarion call, while certainly true, fell on deaf ears. As the embers of the fire cooled, so did the ire of the gay community. In what was to become the dominant pattern of gay activism in New Orleans, the GPC, and *Causeway,* eventually faded away.[61]

SOUTHERN DECADENCE

A year before the Up Stairs Lounge fire, Southern Decadence was born when a close-knit group of friends who playfully called themselves "The Decadents" hosted a small house party. Today the Southern Decadence is one of the largest events in the city's annual calendar, but in 1972, Southern Decadence was merely a way for a handful of bored friends to pass an uneventful weekend. The Decadents gathered regularly at the home of Michael Evers and his lover David Randolph. Several of their fellow Decadents lived in the slave quarters apartment behind the dilapidated house at 2110 Barracks Street in Tremé. Near the front door was a sign that read BELLE REVE, the name of Blanche DuBois's plantation in Tennessee Williams's *A Streetcar Named Desire.*

As Labor Day weekend in 1972 approached, the residents of Belle Reve decided to have a costume party. The theme of the party was "Southern Decadence." Guests were instructed to arrive dressed up as their favorite southern decadent—characters from southern film and literature. About fifty people attended the party, and a good time was had by all. Two weeks later, the Decadents threw a second party, this one to say goodbye to Evers and Randolph, who were about to move out of state. According to Frederick Wright (who two years later would serve as the first Southern Decadence grand marshal), it was "a good party, better than most, but nothing out of the ordinary."[62]

Invitation to the first Southern Decadence party, 1972, designed by Robert Laurent. Courtesy of the authors.

It was good enough for a repeat the following year. In 1973, at Robert Laurent's suggestion, the Belle Reve revelers decided to inaugurate a parade. They began at Johnny Matassa's Grocery & Bar and then marched back to Belle Reve, all the while dressed up as famous southern decadents, including Tallulah Bankhead, Belle Watling, and Mary Ann Mobley. For the third party, Wright was named grand marshal, and the parade route was expanded to include the Golden Lantern, which would in 1981 become the starting point of the parade (and remains so today). As the parade wandered around the lower Quarter, many people spontaneously joined the procession, including the late great Ruthie the Duck Lady. Originally, the parade never had an official route; rather, it meandered around the Quarter at the whim of the grand marshal. This spontaneity was a source of much of the parade's energy and has created some unforgettable moments over the years. In 1986, Grand Marshal Kathleen Conlon led the parade to the Riverwalk, where several drunken revelers jumped in the park fountains, much to the amusement and astonishment of throngs of tourists.

The annual celebration grew slowly each year, and by 1997, 50,000 gay people were coming to New Orleans each Labor Day weekend. The New Orleans Metropolitan Convention and Visitors Bureau began tracking Southern Decadence in that year and estimated the economic impact of the event in 1997 at $25 million. In 2003, Decadence drew over 120,000 visitors and $95 million to the city. By 2010, the number of revelers topped 130,000, with an economic impact of over $160 million. In recent years, Southern Decadence has replaced Mardi Gras as the biggest draw in the city for gay tourists.[63] In recent years, attendance at Southern Decadence numbers over 250,000, with an economic impact of over $300 million.

Many bars in the French Quarter depend on Southern Decadence to boost traditionally slow summer sales; in fact, most of the gay bars in the neighborhood point to Southern Decadence as the source of a hefty percentage of their annual revenue. Café Lafitte is no exception. The bar is usually packed over Labor Day weekend, and the party often spills over into the street. Sometimes the action on the street rivaled or even surpassed the action inside the bars. In 1996, Troy Carter, who was then a member of the city council, observed public sex acts taking place on Bourbon Street outside Café Lafitte in Exile. Somewhat alarmed, Carter called his friend Larry Bagneris, a gay social and political activist who served as the executive director of the mayor's Human Relations Commission and also as an unofficial liaison between the city and the LGBT+ community, and urged him to address the issue of public sex acts during Southern Decadence. Bagneris subsequently reached out to the 1997 Southern Decadence grand marshal, Greg Manogue, also known as "Miss Love," and arranged a meeting with Councilmember Carter to allay his concerns. Manogue and popular bar owner "Miss Fly" met with Carter and obtained the first Southern Decadence parade permit.

The phenomenal growth of Southern Decadence has had a profound impact on the gay community in New Orleans in ways many people do not realize. More specifically, the phenomenal success of Southern Decadence, and its economic impact, revealed to the straight community in New Orleans the spending power of the gay community long before the rest of the country realized that gay people were a powerful economic market with loads of expendable income. Money does not buy acceptance, but it certainly buys a lot of tolerance.

Whatever impact Southern Decadence eventually had on public attitudes toward homosexuality in New Orleans would not be felt until the late 1990s. In the early 1970s, the city was still a very dangerous place for the queer community. Change was in the air for sure, but the great paradigm shift in the way queerness was viewed was decades away. In the meantime, gay and lesbian bars continued to serve the purpose they had for years—namely, providing a place for queer folk to meet, socialize, and have sex. Changes were in the works for Café Lafitte in Exile too. In 1975, Hopkins sold the bar.

4

The Wood Years

TOM WOOD COMES TO TOWN

Thomas G. Wood, the current owner of Café Lafitte in Exile, was born in New Mexico in 1953, the year Café Lafitte in Exile opened. When Wood's father retired, he moved his family to Tulsa, Oklahoma. Young Tom Wood found life in Tulsa boring and longed to be back west. At the age of fifteen, Wood ran away from home and went to Los Angeles. The year was 1968, and Wood self-identified as a hippie. Before long, he was placed in a juvenile hall. Authorities contacted his father, who retrieved him and brought him back to Oklahoma. Eight months later, at the age of sixteen, Wood ran away again. Again, his father retrieved him, and upon returning home, Wood was sent to live with an uncle in Tucson, Arizona. After settling in there, Wood began traveling the nation attending rock music festivals, all the while keeping in touch with his parents and three siblings. He came out to his mother at age eighteen, when she asked him, "Are you like your cousin Gary?" Wood replied, "Yes." His sexual identity was not an issue for his family, and Wood is quick to point out, contrary to the widely held belief, he did not have a traumatic family life.[1]

In 1971, Wood hitchhiked to New Orleans from Boston at the age of seventeen to attend a rock music festival called Festival of Life. Like so many others, he fell in love with New Orleans and decided to stay a while. He got a job at Marti's, a gay-centric restaurant on N. Rampart Street where Tennessee Williams was a regular (Williams lived across the street). Wood didn't work at Marti's long and eventually took a job as a bartender at the Up Stairs Lounge.

Current Café Lafitte in Exile owner Tom Wood, 2024.
Courtesy of the authors.

He struck up a friendship with the Up Stairs owner, Phil Esteve, and remembers, "Phil taught me how to dance."[2]

Wood also supplemented his income with occasional sex work, using the street name Noah. Reflecting on those early days in New Orleans, Wood said: "I was new in town, and I was broke. I did what I had to do."[3] He also pointed out that he has always enjoyed the company of older men, underscoring the fact that working the streets was not a completely unpleasurable experience. Regina Adams remembers Wood working the corner of Bourbon and St. Ann Streets, noting, "Marcy Marcel and I used to buy him beer when we were darting across from the Caverns to Pete's."[4]

By the time an arsonist set fire to the Up Stairs Lounge in 1973, Wood had moved to Florida. There he met a man named Leonard Benton, who went by the name Ben Brown. According to Wood, Brown "wined and dined me."[5] The two developed something of a relationship, and when Brown had to leave town in a hurry, Wood accompanied him. According to Wood, Brown had embezzled some money from the Reynolds Real Estate firm in Fort Myers, Florida, and needed to go on the lam. Brown and Wood fled to New Orleans, where they settled into a relatively comfortable life. Wood found employment at Terry & Juden, a fine men's clothing store on Carondelet Street in the Central Business District, and Brown secured a job at an antique store. The two then began restoring antique clocks and selling them at an auction house in Mississippi. Around this time, a friend of Brown's opened an antique store in Nelson, Missouri, and invited Brown and Wood to join him in the business.

Wood hated Missouri, perhaps because it was reminiscent of Tulsa, and after a year and half, the couple returned to New Orleans. A former manager claims Wood once told him that Brown burned down the antique store to collect the insurance money.

Back in New Orleans, Wood and Brown expressed a desire to buy the Galley House, a popular gay bar in the French Quarter, but their lawyer suggested they buy Café Lafitte in Exile instead because he knew the owner, Tom Hopkins, was ready to sell. Hopkins was indeed eager to sell his business because he owed the Internal Revenue System $20,0000 in back taxes. Brown and Wood were not flush with cash and arranged to finance the purchase. They each became a 50 percent owner in the business and agreed to pay $3,000 a month—$1,500 to Hopkins and $1,500 to the Falgoust family, who owned the building. The bar was only generating about $7,000 a month at the time, and Wood is convinced that Hopkins was hoping they would default on the loan so he could reclaim the business after settling his debt with the IRS.[6]

But Brown and Wood did not default on the loan. The monthly note was expensive, and the bar struggled to turn a marginal profit, but it did. By 1978, Wood discovered Brown had been stealing money from the business and confronted him. Wood offered to buy Brown out, and when Brown initially resisted the offer, Wood threatened to turn Brown into the authorities, saying, "You don't want to go to prison, do you?" Brown, already facing legal trouble on multiple fronts, relented. Wood was now the sole owner of Café Lafitte in

Exile. Wood recalls it took him six months to catch up on all the outstanding bills. Reflecting on Brown, Wood described him as "a con artist."[7]

HOMOPHOBIC CLIMATE

Wood took over Café Lafitte in Exile at a time when homophobia was still rampant and the need for gay spaces was great. The threat of homophobic violence was very real, and queer bars, despite the threat of being raided by the police, offered a somewhat safe space for gay people to congregate. In the spring of 1977, a headline in the *Times-Picayune* read, "Quarterites Ask Protection from Slasher." A serial killer targeting gay men was on the loose in the lower Quarter, and residents were frustrated with police, the article explains. In a two-month span, five men were murdered: Robert Gary, Jack Savell, Alden D. Delano, James McClure, and Ernest Pommier. Sixteen-year-old Warren Harris was eventually arrested for the murders on a tip from two drag queens. During questioning, Harris, who had a trans roommate, spoke of his "revulsion for homosexuals."[8] Harris was convicted in three of the five murders. A severe case of internalized homophobia was apparently the motive in Harris's slaying spree.

Often homophobic violence was not covered in the media. One such incident occurred in 1972. At that time, a handful of gay men met every Friday afternoon for cocktail hour at Pete's, a block away from Lafitte's. One of those men was John Meyers, one of the original bartenders at the Bourbon Pub. At one of the weekly gatherings, John met a fresh face, Jack—a charming young man who was new to the group. On the Saturday of Super Bowl weekend 1972, John was running errands in the Quarter when he ran into Jack at the Lemon Tree, a boutique shop on Royal Street. John greeted Jack, but Jack said nothing. Shrugging his shoulders, John took his leave and went to the A&P grocery store. Again, John saw Jack, and again Jack said nothing. This happened again at a third store. Unsure what to make of Jack's strange behavior, John headed home to his apartment on Chartres Street. Jack was waiting for him outside the building, and this time he spoke: "Johnny, can I come upstairs?" The two proceeded upstairs, and without a word, Jack unzipped John's pants, gave him a blow job, and then left quietly. John recalls, "That surprised me because I didn't think Jack found me attractive."[9]

Twenty minutes later, John heard frantic screaming from the downstairs apartment where his ex-lover Dick Swanson lived with his boyfriend, Chuck. John rushed to the apartment to find Dick lying on the floor bleeding profusely from the chest. Chuck, who had been in the shower, was standing there horrified, and at the kitchen table sat Jack, blank faced, with a bloody knife in his hand. Chuck said, "He's killed the man I wanted to spend the rest of my life with."[10]

John ran back upstairs and called the police, who promptly arrested Jack. John was holding Dick in his arms when he died. Jack was ultimately found to be insane at trial and was committed to a mental institution. Later it was discovered that Jack, under the influence of some exceptionally strong hallucinogenic drugs, had brutally murdered a bartender at one of the gay bars on Iberville Street and chopped the body into pieces the day before he killed Dick. The theory is that he had confessed the crime to Dick and Dick told him he had to turn himself in. Not wanting to hear that, Jack murdered Dick. John remembers Dick's parents coming in from California: "They wanted to see what it was about New Orleans that Dick loved so much. So, I showed them around." John remained friends with them for years, visiting them regularly when he did his medical residency in San Francisco. "They never got over Dick's death."[11]

In the 1970s, Café Lafitte in Exile and a handful of other gay and lesbian bars afforded queer people a place to congregate and meet other like-minded people. There was safety in numbers, but the threat of violence or being outed was still very real. During this time, the only entrance to the bar was on the corner; the two side doors along Bourbon Street remained shuttered. Before exiting the bar, many patrons would gingerly stick their heads out the door and look up and down both Bourbon and Dumaine Streets to make sure no one they knew or worked with would see them leaving a gay bar.

THE BAR'S PERSONALITY

By this point, Café Lafitte in Exile was firmly established as a cruise bar, at least at night. The bar was consistently packed, and many men report having lost their gay virginity in the bar. The crowd was primarily, but not exclusively, middle-aged to older white men and was much more "leathery/denim-ish" than it is now. When the men we interviewed were asked to describe Café Lafitte at that time, typical responses included "skuzzy," "hard-core," "edgy," "lots of action," and "scary" for the uninitiated. Everyone was having sex everywhere: on the pool table, in the bathrooms, in the "blow job corner," and even while sitting at the bar. Before the bar was remodeled, the burlap was riddled with strategically and conveniently cut holes for easy fellatio access. French Quarter fixture Wallace Sherwood, affectionately known as "Wally the Leather Midget," always dressed as a rabbit for the Gay Easter Parade and was a regular fixture "behind the burlap." Some have speculated that Wood replaced the burlap because so many guys were catching crabs from it. Ken Marino remembers: "Café Lafitte in Exile was the first gay bar I ever went to, and it was scary. I was deathly afraid the first time. It was dark, more clandestine than the Burgundy House. We had heard so much about it."[12]

Lloyd Sensat, who was a local artist, historian, and tour guide, remembered Café Lafitte in Exile in the 1970s as "always packed" and "full of action." Like so many people in New Orleans, and especially like so many queer folks, Lloyd was not from New Orleans. He grew up in Crowley, Louisiana, a small town in the southwestern part of the state. He echoed the sentiments of many when he said that even as a small boy, he wanted to live in New Orleans—that he knew he would move to the city someday. After a stint as a teacher in Acadia Parish, he moved to New Orleans in 1976. The pull of the city was strong, and he was encouraged by a friend in Crowley, who told him, "If you want to be happy, you have to leave this small town." That was sage advice, but the sage didn't have the courage to heed his own advice and confessed to Lloyd he planned to marry a girl because, he said, "I don't have the strength."[13]

As a teacher in Crowley, Sensat would come to New Orleans on the weekends and hang out at Café Lafitte in Exile. After moving to the city, his sexuality and creativity flourished. He observed in 2010: "What really attracted me to the city was the architecture and history. Being gay was just a plus."[14] A plus, indeed—especially after serving in the military closet in Korea. With only two months left to serve, Lloyd was caught "in the act" with another man. Perhaps because of his sterling record of service or perhaps because his superior officer was also in the closet, he was admonished to "be more discreet." Lloyd and his partner, Gene Cizek, were together thirty-four years and were a fixture in the Marigny until Lloyd's death in 2011.[15]

Sensat recounted a memorable incident from Lafitte's:

> Gene and I were at one of our local watering holes during Carnival. A new bartender had been brought in for Carnival. We learned that he was a porn star! Last week, he was still in town and working at the bar. He was very friendly, and we were talking. He asked, "Are you from here?" I gave him one of my business cards. He screamed, "Mr. Sensat! You taught me in the sixth grade!" Of course, we discussed everyone that we knew in Luling. There must be something in the water in St. Charles Parish! Isn't it a small world![16]

Sensat wasn't the only teacher to run into a former student at the bar. Darrel Thaxton recalls that while an undergraduate at Southeastern University in Hammond, he and his friends were at Lafitte's on Mardi Gras when Thaxton fell asleep at the bar. When he awoke, he noticed his English professor standing nearby wearing a leather harness and holding a leash that was attached to his partner.[17]

Another patron, Chris, remembers his first visit to Café Lafitte on Halloween night in 1979. He and a friend were walking down Bourbon Street when the friend suggested they duck into Lafitte's to get some poppers. The bar was extremely packed, and the two snaked their way to a back wall near the bathroom. There Chris beheld a man wearing nothing but spiked heels, a jockstrap, and a leather harness standing on a barstool swinging a ball and chain. Chris ran out of the bar "scared as shit" but very intrigued. He returned shortly thereafter and has been a regular since.

In the 1970s, the personality of the bar had changed significantly from past decades. Under Caplinger's ownership decades earlier, Café Lafitte had an artistic centricity, meaning that local artists showcased their works at the bar, and just as many socialized there as well. That gradually changed after the bar relocated to 901 Bourbon and by the 1970s, but despite its reputation as a cruise bar, Wood maintained an artistic sensibility at Lafitte's; the beloved portrait of "Mother," for example, remained a fixture.

One artist whose work Wood enjoyed was George Dureau, whose works he would later display at Good Friends bar. Known primarily for his studies of the nude male figure and black-and-white homoerotic photography, Dureau has

George Dureau, ca. 1970–79. Gift of Donald Dureau,
The Historic New Orleans Collection, acc. no. 2015.0293.1.47.

had exhibits in Paris, London, New York, Los Angeles, and other cities around the United States. For subjects, Dureau looks to the classic male nude in all its chiseled perfection, but he just as often draws upon homeless youths, little people, amputees, the obese, and others who do not conform to mainstream society's traditional standards of beauty. Dureau's frankness of depiction typically brings to life his subjects' beauty and dignity. Classically trained as a painter, Dureau used photographs as studies for his paintings.

For a time, Dureau mentored famed photographer Robert Mapplethorpe, who would come to New Orleans to spend time with and learn from Dureau. Claude Summers has noted that Dureau's photography had a profound influence on Mapplethorpe:

> Dureau's photographs have often been compared with those of Robert Mapplethorpe. But the influence runs not from Mapplethorpe to Dureau but from Dureau to Mapplethorpe. The photographers were friends in the early 1970s. Mapplethorpe was greatly moved by Dureau's photographs, even to the point of restaging many of Dureau's earlier compositions. For all their similarities, however, the photographs of Dureau and Mapplethorpe are quite different. Whereas Mapplethorpe exhibits his subjects as cool and objective, self-contained and remote icons, Dureau presents his as exposed and vulnerable, playful and needy, complex and entirely human individuals. The difference is foremost a matter of empathy.[18]

In 1999, Douglas MacCash, art critic for the *Times-Picayune,* reviewing a Dureau retrospective on display at the Contemporary Arts Center, elaborated on the relationship between Dureau and Mapplethorpe: "In spite of their similar interest in figural photography, the two men found little common ground in their working methods. Mapplethorpe was impatient with Dureau, who spent countless hours conversing with his models, dining, drinking and strolling the French Quarter before he began a photo session. Then he cajoled his models into poses that were partially of his design, but also partially of their making. Why, Mapplethorpe wanted to know, didn't he just pay them and tell them what to do?"[19]

The contrast MacCash paints between the two artists is characteristic of the differences between the two cities in which they grew up, New Orleans and New York, respectively—New York: impersonal, all business and ever in a hurry; New Orleans: friendly, lazy and slow. This affable lethargy is often one of the first qualities of New Orleans that transplants notice when they arrive. Artist Skylar Fein describes it this way: "People here are lulled into a slow, easy life. They want to luxuriate in slow moments. In New York you brag about how busy you are; here you brag about how much time you have."[20]

COMPETITION AND DISCRIMINATION

In the early years of Wood's tenure as owner of Lafitte's, the bar struggled to turn a profit. Part of the reason the bar was not reaching its full profit potential was suggested in a 1977 letter to the *Louisiana Gay Blade,* a statewide newsletter published by Skip Ward: "At the bar on the next corner known by some as 'defeats,' which is a cracker box with no windows and a fireplace. It should have a nice intimate crowd on this cold Monday night. But the music is just too loud to talk to your friends. The bar is anti-social, really. If only half of us had walked out of that bar maybe the owners would get the message."[21] Excessively loud music at the bar would be a constant complaint from bartenders and patrons for decades and persists today. The irony is that Wood used to encourage his bartenders to learn their patrons' names and foster conversation (both with patrons and among themselves)—something impossible to do when the decibel levels are too high. It is not uncommon to see bartenders scurrying to the DJ booth to turn up the volume when they see Wood drive by or approach the bar.

To his credit, there was a time when Wood encouraged his bartenders to facilitate a friendly atmosphere and encouraged them to know patrons by name and introduce them to each other as well as to visitors. For years, there was a sign in the employee break room that read, "What are their names?" One bartender in the 1970s used to write guests' names in chalk on the bar until he remembered them. At many gay bars, bartenders tend to be aloof, if not outright snooty, toward any customer that isn't young or good-looking or doesn't dress "the right way," but that was not the case at Café Lafitte. Former manager Paul Hammond, who was from a casino background, encouraged the bartenders to think of people as guests, not customers. But this hospitality was not extended to everyone. For a long time, Black people and women were not welcomed in the bar.

Racial divisions were sharp in New Orleans in the early 1970s, and most bars, both gay and straight, were segregated. Black gays had far fewer bars than whites; there was the Safari Lounge, Charlie's Corner, and a few others, but many Black gays preferred to socialize in private clubs that met secretly in members' homes. Regina Adams remembers a sign on the door at Café Lafitte in Exile that read, "No Blacks, No Fems, No Women."[22] If a Black gay man had a light enough skin tone—not uncommon among Black Creoles—he could enter the bar by "passing for white." If there was a question over whether the skin tone was light enough, owner Tommy Hopkins would hold up three fingers, a signal to the doorman to require three forms of identification if Hopkins determined the skin tone to be too dark. Longtime regular Tom Cucullu recalls his Black boyfriend in 1967 experiencing the "three finger" treatment.[23]

But if a Black man could "pass for white," he would not be required to produce any identification. Such was the case with John Wilson. "I never had any problems getting into the bars because of my skin color," said Wilson. "I mean, there were people who were friends of mine that knew what I was, but there was no issue made of it because I could be mistaken as white."[24]

Regina Adams, who is white, was dating a Black man named Reginald Adams in 1973 and remembers bringing him to Lafitte's during the day, when there was no doorman. They sat in a rear corner, near the fireplace, out of view of the front door. "He was the first Black man I ever saw drink in Lafitte's," recalled Adams. "And they only let him in because he was with me."[25] Tragically, Reginald Adams died in the Up Stairs Lounge fire later that year.

These discriminatory admittance policies continued after Tom Wood bought the bar. Multiple forms of identification were required of women for entrance. Lesbian Clay Latimer laughingly remembers that was not a problem for her because "they thought I was a boy." One tactic the bar employed to keep lesbians out was to require women to wear dresses. For the most part, this strategy effectively maintained the bar's tradition of men only. In 1986, Kathleen Conlon was grand marshal of Southern Decadence and led the parade (really more of a bar crawl) to Lafitte's and was denied entry. It wasn't until the mid-1990s that women were permitted in the bar without having to produce multiple forms of identification.

When asked later about the bar's admittance policy, Wood responded that it was a different time and he was protecting his customers, noting: "During the '70s, straight women were discouraged from entering the bar. This was dictated by the customers. Women were allowed, but the customers resented it after several people lost their jobs after being outed."[26]

In 1981, this unofficial policy, coupled with the bar's refusal to serve Blacks, resulted in a boycott. At that time, Rich Sacher and Henry Schmidt proposed to the Louisiana Lesbian and Gay Political Action Caucus (LAGPAC) board of directors that it support a boycott against Café Lafitte in Exile and the Bourbon Pub (which had a similar policy). Specifically, the motion was to sign a letter to be published in *Impact* that read: "Are you a bigot? The time has come for the gay community of New Orleans to abolish the blatant sexist and racist discrimination practiced by some of our bars. It is hypocrisy for us to demand our full civil rights from the straight political establishment while we ignore the harassment and humiliation of our fellow gay men and women suffer as their civil rights are violated at the door of the gay bar. We are taking a stand on this issue—will you? How about now?"[27]

The motion failed to pass by a vote of two to five, and LAGPAC declined to join the boycott, a decision that resulted in two directors resigning and flocks of members leaving the organization. Years later, two of the directors who had voted against joining the boycott admitted they were wrong. Wood had initially joined LAGPAC when it was founded in 1980 but quit the organization when it endorsed Jimmy Carter for president.[28]

His penchant for loud music, discriminatory admittance policies, and political views may have all played a role in the bar's declining business after Wood took over, but a more influential factor was the proximity of competing bars. In 1974, popular Lafitte's bartender and manager Jerry Menefee opened the Bourbon Pub one block away from Lafitte's, at the corner of St. Ann Street, with liquor he allegedly stole from Lafitte's. Prior to being the Bourbon Pub, the building at 801 Bourbon housed a bar called the Caverns, a hustler bar known for cheap drugs and even cheaper sex. A former patron recalls: "It was sleazy. But sleazy in a good way." Menefee and his partner, Tex Knight, spent a small fortune renovating the place, and the following year, Menefee bought the building for $140,000.

Menefee was from a prominent family in northern Louisiana, and despite being raised in the midst of that cultural desolation, Menefee was a charismatic figure who had panache and a penchant for extravagant living. Pub bartender Don Wentworth recalls sitting at the bar one day in 1984 when Menefee pulled up in his canary yellow Rolls-Royce, scooped him up, and took him to the airport to pick up Grace Jones and her boyfriend, "a young blonde thing." Jones lip-synched a couple of songs that night at the Pub's tenth anniversary party.

In a 1983 *New York Times* interview, Tex Knight, noted about Menefee: "No one could resist him once he got going. And he was a flamboyant man. He wore tons of jewelry, gold necklaces, rings on every finger, earrings, and enormous hats. You couldn't miss him in a room. No sir!" Menefee died of a heart attack on October 24, 1984, while recuperating from a battle with cancer.

When Menefee opened the Bourbon Pub in 1974, the space across the street that is now Oz was a gay bar called Pete's, the name perhaps playing on the fact that famed jazz clarinetist Pete Fountain had a nightclub there in the 1960s, a fact evidenced by the tiles bearing his name on the sidewalk by the front door. Fountain later moved his club to the Riverside Hilton, where he performed regularly until 2003. After Pete's closed, the space was reincarnated as Le Bistro in 1976. Le Bistro lasted not quite ten years and was the site of the first Miss Gay New Orleans contest. After Le Bistro closed, the space at 800 Bourbon was vacant for a number of years, until Oz opened in 1993.

While the popularity of the Pub and Le Bistro adversely affected Café Lafitte's business, it did serve to establish St. Ann Street as the "lavender line," a demarcation that ultimately benefited Café Lafitte in Exile. And whatever slumps in business the bar suffered, there was always Mardi Gras, which in the 1970s, before Southern Decadence became what it is today, was the premiere holiday for queer folk. Every bar in town—straight or gay—benefited from Mardi Gras, of course, but Lafitte's had something other bars did not: the Bourbon Street Awards.

Started in 1964 by Arthur Jacobs, owner of the Clover Grill, as a way to drum up business for his diner, the Bourbon Street Awards has grown into an internationally known feature of Mardi Gras. But this success belies the

Crowds await the Bourbon Street Awards at Café Lafitte in Exile, 1968.
Photo by Joe Crews, courtesy Louisiana State Museum.

contest's humble origins. According to Jacobs: "That's when I thought of a Mardi Gras costume contest right outside the grill. I figured if I could get people to come to the contest, they'd buy some food once they got there and maybe come back. But I didn't think of it as anything more than a one-time thing."[29] Jacobs's idea was a hit, and the contest became an annual Mardi Gras tradition. Jacobs produced the contest until 1973, when he turned it over to Café Lafitte in Exile.

At that time, local legend Edd Smith began hosting the show. He quickly became known as "Mr. Bourbon Street Awards," and the contest continued to grow in popularity, featuring three hundred contestants in 1977 alone. The show's success enabled Café Lafitte to make up for whatever business may have been taken away by the other bars down the street. In 1977, the *Times-Picayune* noted the boom to business that was the Bourbon Street Awards: "At the junction of Bourbon and Dumaine Streets, the Mardi Gras crowd is invariably dozens of bodies deep. Necks are craned and cameras trained toward the stage outside the entrance to Café Lafitte in Exile, a busy bar. All year long high-priced tickets are sold to Lafitte's upstairs bar and balcony, from which the view of the stage is prime . . . 'According to wholesale liquor dealers here,' explains veteran contest emcee, 'Café Lafitte has the largest liquor account year around, next to Pat O'Briens."[30]

For his fifth anniversary hosting the contest, the bar presented Edd Smith a 24-karat gold hard hat with a sterling silver plate on the front that read, "Café Lafitte's Mascot, Edd Smith."

Over the decades, the Bourbon Street Awards have had a variety of celebrity hosts, including Varla Jean Merman, Blanche Debris, and Bianca del Rio. "Actually, it's a lot of headaches, tons of red tape and paperwork, endless man-hours dealing with permits and City Hall." Tom Wood observed in a 1996 interview. "But people love it. I must confess I wake-up Mardi Gras morning and think 'Damn! We have to do the contest.' But even I enjoy it after it gets going. I mean, some of the costumes are pretty hysterical. It's a showcase for a lot of clever work. And besides, where are those drag queens gonna go?"[31]

Wood Enterprises still owns the Bourbon Street Awards, but the contest is no longer held outside Café Lafitte in Exile; in recent years, the costume contest has been held on St. Ann Street near Wood's other bars, Good Friends and Rawhide. Lafitte's, like most French Quarter bars, still benefits from Mardi Gras. In addition to increased business, the intersection where the bar is located is also a favorite stop for the fundamentalist, evangelical Christians, who come to Mardi Gras (and Southern Decadence) every year equipped with bullhorns and large signs that proclaim "God Hates Fags" and lists of people who are "going to hell": Catholics, vegetarians, onanists, New Agers, skateboarders, gamblers, pot smokers, boozers, and people who do yoga. These street preachers are very aggressive in their attempt to "save souls."

A PIVOTAL YEAR

The year 1978 was a pivotal year in the bar's history and in Wood's personal life. By 1978, the bar was solely under Wood's ownership. In an effort to increase business, Wood gave the upstairs a facelift. He had opened a restaurant upstairs called the Streetcar. The bar was staffed by a colorful character, Robert "Miss Pratt" Prattini. The Streetcar was not open long. Ken Marino, who waited tables there briefly, recalls, "It lasted a month maybe."[32]

Wood removed the kitchen and converted the restaurant into a bar called the Corral, which had a western motif. Wood recalls opening the Corral with virtually no money, noting that they had to scour abandoned lots for materials.[33] The Corral lasted a dozen years or so, but after the name went away, the upstairs area continued to function and is today called the Balcony Bar. It was also in 1978 that Wood met Jerry Morgan.

Morgan was a lieutenant colonel in the U.S. Marine Corps stationed in Louisville, Kentucky. Originally from Maine, he had previously lived in New Orleans and would visit often. On one of those occasions, he and a friend, Clyde Webb, were drinking at Café Lafitte in Exile, when he met Wood. The two hit it off and became friends and then lovers. Wood visited Morgan in Kentucky and convinced him to move to New Orleans. The Marine Corps was not happy when Morgan decided to retire and threatened him with a dishonorable discharge for being gay. Wood says the Marine Corps had launched an investigation and was surprised that Morgan was spending so much time with Wood, despite being married. Wood met with marine attorneys, and a settlement of sorts was reached; Morgan would be discharged from military service honorably. Morgan's wife knew about Morgan's relationship with Wood and maintained a friendship with both men. Morgan and Wood lived together in a house on the lakefront, while Morgan's wife lived in Pensacola, Florida. Morgan was not an owner in the bar but was a constant presence there, which led many to believe he was a co-owner. Morgan and Wood were not business partners but, rather, life partners. Morgan died of a heart attack outside of his home in 1983 as he and Wood were jogging. Morgan's wife, to whom he was still legally married at the time of his death, attended his memorial service in the French Quarter.[34]

In 1979, Wood began expanding his business empire. In that year, he opened an upscale bar with a western motif called the Great American Refuge on the corner of Royal and Ursulines Streets in the French Quarter. Wood owned the bar less than ten years, eventually selling it to rival bar owner Jerry Menefee.

In 1982, Wood and Morgan were involved in a police incident at Lafitte's that resulted in yet another civil lawsuit. On February 26, 1982, the Thursday

The staff of Café Lafitte in Exile in 1981. Jerry Morgan is at the *center of the bottom row.* Tom Wood is to the *right* of Morgan. Courtesy of the authors.

before Mardi Gras, four New Orleans police officers responded to a complaint at the bar regarding drugs and obscenity. Around 11:30 p.m., New Orleans police officers Scanlon and Britt arrived at the bar and rushed upstairs. When Wood tried to speak with the police, the last two officers to arrive told Wood to "Get out of the way, you (expletive deleted) faggot." The incident resulted in a civil trial, at which Wood testified that Officer Britt had shoved him against a wall and began beating him with his nightstick: "They struck me seven, eight, nine times and I kept wondering if they were going to kill me. I could hear the hits against my head, and I could hear flesh tearing." Morgan witnessed the incident and testified at the trial: "They pushed him down and proceeded to beat the hell out of him with their billy-clubs."[35] Wood's suit requested $590,750 in compensatory damages and $300,000 in punitive damages. The jury, four men and two women, awarded Wood $7,500 after deliberating only two hours.

POLICE AND POLITICS

There was no love lost between Wood and the New Orleans Police Department. In the 1960s and early 1970s, the police would show up at Lafitte's at the same time each week to collect an envelope stuffed with cash from the bartender. In exchange, the police would, for the most part, leave the bar alone. Wood stopped making the payments when he took over the bar and eventually obtained a restraining order against the police because of their harassment.

The queer community's relationship with police was still very hostile in 1981. Two months after assaulting Wood in his own bar, the New Orleans Police Department conducted what they called a "sidewalk sweep" outside of several gay and lesbian bars, including Jewel's, Diane's, and the Grog. Numerous people were arrested for obstructing the sidewalk. The mass arrests led to the creation of the Crescent City Coalition (CCC). One of CCC's founding members, Roger Nelson, remembers the organization "grew out of a feeling in our community with the surfacing of police harassment that we needed a more active and community accountable civil rights organization than LAGPAC had been to that date."[36] Both LAGPAC and CCC worked tirelessly, and often collaboratively, to educate the police department concerning queer issues and thereby improve the relationship between the police and the LGBT+ community. Their efforts would eventually cause the police department to abandon its long-standing practice of utilizing "field interrogation cards," basically index cards on which they would take notes after arbitrarily stopping people on the street who they thought looked like gay men or lesbians. Nevertheless, it would be decades before police attitudes shifted significantly.

In 1981, Mayor Ernest "Dutch" Morial established a Public Education Task Force to look into problems in the gay community. Gay political activists from that era agree Morial was the first mayor who demonstrated any support for the gay community and the first mayor to meet with the community. Attorney Jack Sullivan recalls the meeting: "Dutch gave a very supportive speech, and the one line I'll always remember is him saying, 'As long as I'm mayor, no one will ever be discriminated against because of his sexual "affectation."'"[37]

During Mayor Morial's tenure in the 1980s, a significant change occurred within the police department. The Mayor's Advisory Commission began conducting sensitivity training at the police academy. This training essentially consisted of gay men and women recounting for cadets their own experiences as gay citizens, including personal accounts of harassment. Those who told their stories agree the training was an overall positive step in the right direction, yet they all concede that reactions among the recruits were decidedly mixed.

While the 1980s witnessed a flurry of queer organizing, antidiscrimination laws would take another decade to materialize. In 1991, the City Council finally passed a proposal to include "sexual orientation" as a protected category in an antidiscrimination ordinance. Two years later, the city enacted a domestic partnership ordinance; Rip and Marsha Naquin-Delain, regulars at Lafitte's and publishers of *Ambush Magazine,* were the first in line to register as domestic partners. Five years after passing the ordinance, the city council amended the 1991 statute to add "gender identity" as a recognized, protected class. New Orleans was one of the first American cities to do so. In 1997, Mayor Marc H. Morial extended domestic partner benefits to city employees. In recognition of the long-standing contributions gays and lesbians have made to New Orleans, the city announced an outreach program designed to entice gays to move to New Orleans. Also in 1999, a state appeals court struck down (temporarily) Louisiana's long-standing sodomy law, enacted in 1805, which criminalized oral and anal sex.

In spite of the legal strides made by the gay community in the 1990s, a homophobic relic from previous decades reared its ugly head in 1998: the good old-fashioned police raid of a gay bar. Two days before Southern Decadence, police raided the Phoenix, a leather bar in the Marigny, and arrested fourteen men, including the bar manager, who was charged with permitting sexual acts to occur in a public facility that serves alcohol.

By the 1990s, public attitudes toward homosexuality had begun to change for the better. In 1990, Angela Hill of television station WWL hosted a week-long special series on the gay community in New Orleans. The five episodes each featured an aspect of LGBT+ life: What is homosexuality? Do gay people in New Orleans face discrimination? Should gay people be allowed to marry? What are the common misconceptions of lesbianism? and lastly, What problems do gay teens face? Each show featured three to five guests, who answered questions from Hill and then the audience. At the end of the decade and in the early 2000s, the phenomenal growth of the annual Southern Decadence festival after the advent of the internet also helped shift attitudes in New Orleans. As more and more out-of-town revelers visited each Labor Day weekend, the city realized the untapped spending power of the gay community. Money may not buy acceptance, but it can buy a lot of tolerance. But in the 1970s, Southern Decadence was still a smallish affair, and the queer tourist market was still in the closet, and homophobia was still de rigueur.

VIOLENCE REARS ITS UGLY HEAD

A serial killer targeting gay men in the French Quarter surfaced in 1984. Early in that year, five men were bludgeoned with a hammer, three of whom died: Gene Davis, owner of Gregory's and formerly Wanda's and Gene's Hideaway; Paul Egan, maintenance manager for the Gunga Den; Bruce Richardson, former owner of Fat Sam's; Jerry Beeson, bartender at the Galley House; and John Hooper, regular patron of the Golden Lantern. All were attacked in their homes. The killer was never apprehended, and the murders remain unsolved.

In 1988, thirty-two-year-old Floyd Wright, of Compton, California, fired several shots from a .45 caliber handgun into Café Lafitte from the front door. Patrons at the bar tackled Wright and held him until police arrived and arrested him for attempted murder. No one was wounded in the incident.

Homophobia was the motive in another high-profile murder in 1993. Early one Thursday morning in November, twenty-three-year-old Joseph Balog and a friend were walking down Dauphine Street, when they were attacked by four men who taunted them with gay slurs. Balog and his friend were not gay, but that didn't matter to the vicious mob. Balog was stabbed in the chest, back, and hand and was found lying on the sidewalk of St. Philip Street between Dauphine and Bourbon. A Quarter resident out walking his dog found Balog bleeding to death and barely conscious. He was rushed to Charity Hospital, where he died. His friend managed to escape the bloody attack. The following night, Lin-Todd Soldani organized a rally and candlelight march to the location of the murders. Police arrested Ronald Graves for the murder, but at trial the jury deadlocked.

In 2007, Robin Malta, a former manager at Café Lafitte and credited (along with Errol Rizzuto) as having founded the annual Red Party charity event at the bar in 1994, was murdered. At the time of his death, Malta owned a popular hair salon in the French Quarter. He and Rizzuto both worked at Café Lafitte and had both served as Southern Decadence grand marshals.

BRICKS AND MORTAR

Throughout all the homophobia of the 1970s and 1980s, Café Lafitte in Exile remained a constant, fixed star in the ever-shifting constellation of French Quarter gay bars. In 1986, Wood initiated major renovations to the bar. The burlap decor was replaced with mahogany, which is still in use today. At the time, the pole in the center of the area behind the bar was adorned with shelves to hold liquor, but the shelves were scrapped, and the bottles were moved to wells and shelves underneath the bar. A billiards table was added to the upstairs bar, and Marc Marino painted a wall mural featuring the bar's regulars. To the chagrin of many, this mural would later be lost in a future renovation. The bar did not close during the renovation, and when it was completed, the interior of the bar looked much as it does today. Wood eventually persuaded the owner of the building to sell, and in 1994, Wood purchased the building, thus ensuring Café Lafitte in Exile would have a permanent home. After the purchase, a huge party was thrown to celebrate, and Wood burned the old lease in the eternal flame. The ashes are kept in a twenty-ounce go-cup in the bar's office. Café Lafitte in Exile was home for good.

In 1995, Wood raised the ire of neighborhood residents and French Quarter preservationists when he applied for a permit to install a covered roof over the gallery of the bar. Neighbors opposed the idea, citing increased noise, and circulated a petition against the proposal. Wood responded with a petition of his own and hand-delivered a personal letter he had penned to opponents of the roof. One sentence in the letter caused alarm: "We are glad for your participation and involvement in the community, and we are glad to know who you (are) and where you live." Many interpreted this as a threat, which only exacerbated the tension. Wood wrote a letter to the Vieux Carré Commission (VCC) arguing that opposition to the roof stemmed from homophobia. "As for those who long for the days when our community was closeted behind closed doors and shutters, I have only pity," Wood wrote. "Is this issue really about noise and architecture, or our increasing visibility?"[38] Ultimately, the VCC voted five to one to reject Wood's application.[39] Wood applied for a rooftop over the gallery again twenty-five years later but was again denied.

Roof or not, many regulars preferred the balcony bar to downstairs because it tended to be quieter and less crowded. One regular patron named Louis recalls the music at the balcony bar being not as loud as it was downstairs: "You could actually talk to people upstairs. It was a great spot for conversation. And sex. We used to have a lot of sex upstairs, but that was usually on the weekend or for Mardi Gras."[40]

There is something special about French Quarter balconies, and the balcony at Lafitte's is no exception. Multitudes of men have recounted for us memorable escapades on the balcony, especially during Mardi Gras and Decadence weekends. Typically, on those weekends, dark sheets are draped over the ironwork in order to somewhat conceal what can justifiably be described as an orgy of fellatio. Before Katrina, the balcony bar was open all week long; now it is only open on the weekends. Often the balcony serves as a tranquil respite from the hustle and bustle of the main bar. Scotty, a longtime regular, says the balcony is his favorite spot in the city when it's not crowded:

> More than anything, I feel peace when I'm there. Sometimes Michael and I go there to sit and talk and relax and people-watch. I remember once I had a very stressful day at work, and Michael said to me, "You need the

> balcony. Let's go to Lafitte's." So, we went to unwind. It's so beautiful when the sun is setting. The taller, more modern buildings of the Central Business District silhouette the Spanish architecture of the buildings immediately before you. On that night, above the skyscrapers, the stars seemed to dance around a not-quite-crescent moon, and I totally zoned out. Michael waved his hand in front of my face to bring me back to earth and then asked me where I was. Then I was reminded why they call New Orleans "The City That Care Forgot."[41]

CRUISING

Jeffrey Palmquist remembers his first Southern Decadence as a bartender at Café Lafitte:

> I was new so I got a shit assignment—the balcony bar. But it was okay for Decadence because it was packed. This guy standing at the bar was drinking a Bud Light and talking to his friends. When he ordered another beer, I asked him if he needed anything else. The guy reaches down and grabs another by the hair and pulls him to eye level with the bar and says, "Want anything?" The guy on his knees nods no, and his head disappeared. Until then, it had never occurred to me the man standing had been getting a blow job the whole time. I soon learned that was very common.

Sex in the bar is not as common as it used to be, but it occasionally still occurs, primarily during Mardi Gras and Southern Decadence weekends. These trysts almost always occur upstairs, but every now and then, raw lust manifests downstairs as well. David, a bartender, recalls showing up for his shift to see the entire bar fixated by a drunken drag queen "taking it up the ass by a big trucker dude" near the DJ booth. Likewise, Palmquist remembers a similar incident from a few years ago: "The bar was fairly busy and kind of noisy. Then, as I was mixing drinks, I heard what sounded like applause, only it wasn't. By the fireplace, somebody was getting fucked so hard that the thrusts against his ass sounded like hands clapping."[42]

All this gay sex was just too much for some Christians to take. During Mardi Gras weekend in 1996, the street preachers provoked Tom Wood to retaliatory action that resulted in a civil lawsuit. According to court records, a man named Jonas Robertson was standing at or near the entrance to Café Lafitte in Exile with a bullhorn, loudly proclaiming that homosexuality was a sin and that everyone in the bar was going to hell unless they repented and gave their lives to Jesus. Wood responding by retrieving a hose and spraying Robertson with water. Wood claimed he was aiming the hose at the megaphone to "short it out," a fact belied by the fact that Wood sprayed Robertson for thirty minutes.[43] Wood also claimed he was trying to disperse the crowd in the street in order to prevent a riot. Ultimately, the incident became physical, when Wood punched Robertson in the shoulder.

In the mid-1990s, a local pastor, the Reverend Grant Storms, began protesting Southern Decadence. But more than simply protesting, Storms went into the gay bars and surreptitiously filmed random sex acts being performed and went to the local media with the tape. The local news stations ran stories on the issue, but the city, for the most part, shrugged and soon forgot about it. Then the national media got wind of the story, and the city and the bars were compelled to respond, at least perfunctorily. This is why most gay bars in New Orleans had for years (before the advent of cell phones) a no cameras / no photography policy. Reverend Storms eventually faded away into obscurity until he resurfaced rather dramatically in 2011, when he was arrested for masturbating at a children's park in Metairie.

The bar's reputation as a cruise bar runs deep. Longtime regular Louis wryly observes, "Before the Phoenix, before Jewel's, there was Lafitte's." In the late 1960s and early 1970s, Lafitte's was "the only leather/Levi's bar in town . . . and they didn't have any twink bartenders back then. They came later." Louis recalls:

> Back then, business pretty much dictated your private life. You'd see men at Lafitte's at night wearing denim and tees or leather or sometimes nothing at all, but during the day, these same guys wore conservative suits and played it straight. One guy I used to hang out with is still a member of Rex. The place was always packed. How the Fire Department never shut

the place down is beyond me. There was always a lot of feeling and groping. Clusters of naked men would gather in corners or in the bathroom. There would be piles of clothes along the wall or near barstools, but no one worried about them being stolen because we all knew each other, and we looked out for each other.

Hustlers didn't come to Lafitte's because so much ass was being given away for free. It wasn't worth their time. There was this one kid, though, I do remember. He must have been in junior high, and he'd hustle on the corner right outside the Clover Grill. The bouncers wouldn't let him in because he was too young. Nobody really paid much attention to IDs then, but I guess they had to draw the line somewhere. Anyway, the regulars at Lafitte's used to watch out for him and bring him Cokes. He may have gotten some business from the bar, but I think it was mostly closeted men who would drive by and pick him up.

I had grown up on the West Bank and in Mid-City near City Park. I knew I was gay when I was around eleven or twelve years old, but I acted straight. Everyone did back then. We were all so scared. I was even engaged for a while. When we went out, I couldn't wait to drop her off at her house after the date and go to Lafitte's. I must have been twenty-one the first time I went. One time, I was with a group of friends in the Quarter, and we ended up at Lafitte's, and we all acted like we didn't know it was a gay bar, which seems kind of silly now. When we left, one of them said loudly, acting surprised, "Man, that was a gay bar!" Oh, and I once ran into my cousin at Lafitte's. When he asked me what I was doing there, I said, "The same thing you are."

I never did get married; I liked to play around too much. I still love chicken.[44]

Fueling much of the sexual activity at the bar was cocaine. Stories of drug use at the bar are legion. One we heard repeatedly concerned Joel Hoffman, who used to hide coke under his wig while he tended the bar in the mid-1990s. Hoffman went on to meet a tragic end, eventually overdosing from shooting up. Sadly, his body was found lying on the floor of an adult bookstore. One DJ in the 1990s sold coke out of the DJ booth, but that little enterprise ended when the police came looking for him. They arrived at shift change, and he was in the back of the house. Upon being alerted of their arrival, he hid in the walk-in cooler. The police, not realizing it was shift change, interrogated the DJ, who had just come on duty. This DJ, not having anything to fear, answered all their questions and readily allowed them to search his bag. The police didn't find any coke, but they did find a bundle of joints, which the poor DJ had completely forgotten about. Both DJs were arrested. Several bartenders used to openly snort rails of coke on the bar, as did some patrons. Robbie and Herbie, a couple that frequented the bar in the early 1980s, remember doing poppers at the bar one night when one of them dropped the bottle on the floor. As they crouched down, Robbie lit a cigarette lighter to look for the wayward bottle. In the process, the burlap caught fire, though it was quickly extinguished and did not cause significant damage. Regulars who were around then universally agree drugs were available everywhere.

Sometimes random hookups led to meaningful relationships. Bill, a twenty-five-year regular at Lafitte's, grew up in a small town on Bayou Lafourche, about an hour outside of New Orleans. When he was a senior in high school, Bill went to Lafitte's and fell in love with the place; it was his first gay bar. As a veteran of the gay scene in New Orleans, Bill has been to many gay bars, but he always stayed loyal to Lafitte's: "When I first started coming to New Orleans on the weekends, I checked a lot of bars and clubs. I liked Lafitte's because it wasn't pretentious. It wasn't trendy, and it wasn't spur of the moment. It just was. And it still is."[45]

Bill met David during Mardi Gras 2008. David, a local who had grown up in Metairie, saw Bill across the bar and sent him a drink. Then he went over and introduced himself. In a matter of moments, the two were upstairs on the "meat rack." After an especially memorable blow job, they decided to see each other again and have been together ever since.

AIDS

One influence that discouraged public cruising and sex in the bar in the 1980s was the emerging AIDS epidemic. Because of New Orleans's popularity as a tourist destination and as an international port, HIV probably arrived in the city in the late 1970s, but the full scope of the AIDS crisis did not grip the local community until the mid-1980s.[46] The men we interviewed for this book who were around then found this issue the most difficult to talk about. Some refused to discuss it at all. Just as many broke down in tears as they remembered those they had lost. All conveyed the same sense of sadness and horror. Many mournfully recalled "going to too many funerals." Longtime Lafitte's bartender Wilhelmina summed up everyone's feelings by simply stating, "It was a very, very difficult time." Wilhelmina estimates he lost "at least" one hundred friends and acquaintances to AIDS:

> It was so bad you were afraid to answer your phone. I remember throwing away my address book because most everyone in it had died. It was horrible. No one knew what was going on and everyone was fearful. Charity Hospital had a separate floor for AIDS patients. Orderlies would set patients' meals outside the doors in the hall for fear of being in the same room with someone infected. And visitors were forced to wear masks and gowns. You'd go to the hospital to visit a friend and be shocked at how sickly they looked but also at how many other people you knew who were also patients. After a while, it took a heavy toll on me. I became cold.[47]

As he rattled off name after name of those who had died, Wilhelmina paused at the mention of his friend Rodger Garber. His voice cracked, and tears began to form in his eyes. "I'm sorry. I need a moment," he told us. Rodger had been a childhood friend in Ohio who eventually followed him to New Orleans. In 1988, Rodger suddenly disappeared. He had moved home to die within days of testing positive. As the disease progressed and his health declined, he called Wilhelmina and asked him to come visit him in Ohio. Upon arriving, Rodger's mother warned him of Rodger's ghastly appearance so he wouldn't freak out when he saw him. The warning was futile. Rodger was pale and gaunt and thin, his face sunken into his skull, much of its skin eaten away by the meds (AZT). Wilhelmina lost it. After regaining his composure, they visited and reminisced and laughed and cried. Rodger was a huge Bette Midler fan and told Wilhelmina, quoting the singer, "You'll always be the wind beneath my wings." He died a few days later.

Jerry Hocke, Albert Carey's partner of seventeen years, succumbed to the disease in 1989, three years after being diagnosed. Reflecting on that dark time, Carey recalls:

> Jerry was a veteran (he had a bum leg due to a mortar attack in Vietnam) so he died at the VA hospital. The staff wouldn't even go into the room. They would set his tray of food on the floor in the hall right by the door. I'd bring it in and feed him. There really weren't any treatment options then. The only drug that seemed promising was AZT, and that was $900 for a month's supply. We heard of some drug the FDA had not yet approved but it was available in Mexico. I even went down there to get some, but it didn't work. Of course, in that predicament, you try anything.[48]

The ramifications of the AIDS outbreak were utterly devastating to the gay community in New Orleans, especially since it was such an intimate community. The toll was especially hard on the gay Carnival krewes. New Orleans has always been a big small town, with the French Quarter an even smaller village unto itself. In years past, before over-tourism began to ravage the neighborhood, the Quarter had a close-knit neighborhood feel; everyone—neighbors and bartenders and shopkeepers—knew each other. This camaraderie was even more tightly woven among the gay community. This parochial bond made the AIDS outbreak seem much more intense and acute than it did in larger cities. Everyone knew people who had died, or were dying, and no one knew exactly why. Nor did anyone know how to handle the crisis. Widespread public ignorance of the nature of the disease, particularly how it spread, caused a lot of fear. Paranoia and sadness ruled the day. Dr. Jody Gates, a lesbian and the administrator of a hospital at the time, remembers the struggle to keep up with the latest laws and treatment recommendations. "The most important thing," she recalls, "was to not let people panic."[49]

The gay community's reaction to the crisis was as diverse as the community itself. Some men went back into the closet, while others vowed to be celibate. Some questioned all the strides made in the previous decade, and some even bought into the conservative Right's rhetoric of divine judgment. Shame and fear were common reactions. Just as common was a renewed determination to fight on for equality and dignity. Doctors refused to see patients they knew were gay until they were tested. Police used masks and gloves when arresting known gay people.

Legendary performer Marcy Marcel hosted the first AIDS fundraiser in New Orleans in 1984, raising about $350. Marcy recalls, "I was at an Uptown party when CNN broke the story of a gay disease. We had no idea it would be as bad as it was."[50]

Those infected also reacted in different ways. Some who became infected turned their anger into vengeance and tried to infect as many others as possible. Many went home to die. Some, those who had no home to go home to, moved in with friends for their final days. Others went to die at Lazarus House, the first AIDS hospice in New Orleans (founded in 1985) and the oldest facility offering assisted living to AIDS patients in the Gulf Region. According to Wilhelmina, one victim, Patrick Kelly, decided to make the most of his remaining time by maxing out his credit cards and traveling the world. Others became hysterically convinced the virus was created and spread by the government to rid society of homosexuality. In addition to the home operated by Project Lazarus, other organizations emerged to help fight the disease, notably the NO/AIDS Task Force (now known as Crescent Care), Belle Reve and Trinity House (residential assisted living facilities), Southeastern Louisiana AIDS Awareness, the New Orleans Regional AIDS Planning Council, New Orleans Women Against AIDS, Art Against Aids, ACT UP, and others.

For his part, Wilhelmina transformed his grief into the strength required to reconcile with his father. One day in 1986, he showed up unexpectedly on his parents' doorstep and told his father firmly, "This ends now because it's only hurting Mom." Father and son embraced and began the process of restoring their relationship.

Despite the devastation and heartache the AIDS crisis engendered, it did have one positive effect that is often overlooked: it humanized the gay community, which in turn affected many straight people's view on queerness. Looking back, Jack Sullivan observed, "AIDS forced so many people out of the closet, the mainstream establishment realized, 'Oh, I didn't know you were gay.' AIDS created a forced visibility."[51] Assessing the epidemic in hindsight, local businessman and former journalist Eric Hess observed simply, "AIDS changed everything."[52]

Tom Wood muses: "I think AIDS brought a lot of people to the forefront, and the general population was forced to accept our existence. We were allowed to open our doors on the Bourbon Street side."[53] Wood's involvement in the community's response to the AIDS crisis was minimal. In 1987, he hosted a cocktail party for volunteers who worked with the NO/AIDS Task Force, and he occasionally donated food and supplies for the group's fundraisers. Wood Enterprises also supported the No/AIDS Walk in 1990 by purchasing an ad in the program.

WOODCHIPS

One consistent feature of the bar under Wood's tenure as owner has been an incredibly high turnover rate, especially among bar managers. One former general manager of Wood Enterprises estimates Lafitte's goes through, on average, one manager a year. The number of recycled bartenders is also high. Several managers were petty larcenists, one even leaving a note in the safe on his last night that read, "I stole $400. Bye." And one manager in the early 1990s routinely raided the bartender's cash drawers to fund his cocaine habit. Several men we interviewed told us of a bartender who stole "a lot of money" and allegedly fled to Brazil. Of the hundreds of bartenders who came and went at Lafitte's over the years, a few names came up repeatedly in our interviews—Alabama Jim, Billy Bayou, and Floyd. In addition to serving drinks, Floyd also orally serviced patrons, and he wasn't the only one. For a while, bartenders upstairs worked in the nude.

There are a few notable exceptions to the traditionally high turnover rate. One of this book's authors, Jeffrey Palmquist, for example, worked as a bartender at Lafitte's for twenty-four years. And Aletha Bryant began working in the bar as a cleaning person before becoming a bartender. Bryant worked at Lafitte's for decades. She was ultimately fired for allegedly stealing a poker bank ($1,500). Wood pressed charges, but Bryant was acquitted at trial.

The universal testimony of Wood's former employees is that he was a boss for whom it was not easy to work. When asked why, the typical answers include his unreasonable demands, racism, ageism, misogyny, transphobia, a general disdain for feminine men, and Wood's political views, which lean heavily to the hard Right. (Wood was a founding member of the New Orleans chapter of the Log Cabin Republicans in 1992. Today he claims to be registered as an independent.) Many of these employees chose to quit and work elsewhere, but just as many were fired. According to a former manager, one of the first things Wood instructs newly hired managers to do is choose a bartender to fire to "let the other employees know who's boss." Those employees who were fired, justifiably or not, are so numerous that they jokingly refer to themselves as "woodchips."

Many former employees (and patrons) relate horror stories about Wood's treatment of his employees. For example, Wood told one bartender, "I own you." The bartender replied, "No, you don't," and walked out the door, never to return. Sometimes, when drunk, Wood would get angry and violent with the bartenders. Harry Hodges, who bartended at Lafitte's in the early 1980s, remembers Wood getting angry with him because he wasn't "flirting enough with the customers" and threw a glass ashtray at him.[54] On another occasion, he threw a barstool at popular Good Friends bartender Spencer Cortez. Other former employees recall Wood urinating in go-cups at the bar and handing the cups to a bartender to throw away—something Wood vehemently denies. And once at the Clover Grill, on a holiday when the diner was packed, Wood showed up with people he wanted to impress and told the short-order cook, "I don't care who the next three hamburgers are for, they're for me."

Elizabeth Lanoix worked briefly at Café Lafitte in Exile as a cleaning person and recalls Wood forcing her to mop the floor over twenty times in a row because she wasn't "doing it correctly." Lanoix was convinced Wood was deliberately tormenting her because she believed he hated women.[55] Lanoix was not alone in this belief.

Another complaint against Wood was that he did not want drag queens or feminine men working behind the bar. Shane Scallan was hired as a bartender but was fired during his first shift, when Wood entered the bar, noticed his feminine demeanor, and told the manager, "I want that thing gone tonight."[56]

In 2007, a former manager at the bar sued Wood Enterprises for what he alleged was age discrimination. William Bryan, better known as "Billy Bayou," worked on and off as a bartender at Café Lafitte in Exile from the early 1980s until Hurricane Katrina forced him to relocate outside of New Orleans. The following year, he returned to New Orleans and was hired to be the bar manager at Lafitte's. In January 2007, he was fired and subsequently sued the business. Wood Enterprises claimed he was fired for violating company policy, which prohibits managers from doing back-office work during a bartending shift. The company also claimed Bryan once left the bar in the hands of an unlicensed trainee, thus violating the Municipal Code, which requires a manager with a permit to sell alcohol to be on the premises at all times. Bryan did not dispute those facts but claimed the real reason he was fired was because of his age (he was forty-nine). In court documents, Bryan cited comments by the corporate office staff joking about his age, referring to him as "grandpa" and "old man." Bryan further claimed the general manager of Wood Enterprises instructed him not to schedule himself for weekend bartending shifts because "Mr. Wood want[ed] a younger look behind the bar."[57] Ultimately, the case was dismissed on summary judgment. Bryan reportedly told a former manager he was not upset his case was dismissed and that he was glad Wood had to spend $100,000 defending the case.

Not all of Wood's former employees share these negative sentiments. Ken Marino, a former general manager, noted, "Tom was the most generous man I've ever met." Marino met Wood as a customer at the bar in 1977. At the time, Marino was a loan officer at the Bank of New Orleans. Wood was banking with Whitney Bank, and Marino wanted his business, which he eventually won over. The two became friends, and Marino eventually began working as relief help on Sundays, making banks and processing deposits at Café Lafitte in Exile. He also worked as a bartender at the Refuge and was eventually promoted to general manager, a position he held until 2001. When asked about former employees who had less than favorable impressions of Wood, Marino said, "They didn't know him." He added, "Tom is very loyal if he respects you."[58] Wood's generosity is also evidenced in the fact he sent a former lover (Poppy) monthly checks after they were no longer together. One former manager also said Wood wanted to give him a raise but didn't want the comptroller and other office staff to know, so he secretly gave him $5,000 in cash.

But despite these examples of generosity, the general consensus among former employees is that Wood views his employees as dispensable. He maintained a distance from bartenders and earned a reputation for nonchalantly firing them. When asked about former employees who had been fired and their criticism of him, Wood responded, "Losers always have excuses."[59] With managers, he was more circumspect. More than one former manager observed that Wood's modus operandi when he wanted to get rid of a manager was to make their lives miserable until they quit, a method that didn't always work.

Although not known for his benevolence, Wood Enterprises engages in charitable giving. For years, one of the more popular charity events in the French Quarter was the Red Party, hosted annually by Café Lafitte. In 1993 or

1994, manager Robin Malta and employee Errol Rizzuto started the event, perhaps in response to the nationally renowned White Party, a weeklong circuit party held each year in Palm Springs. Each year, the Red Party raised around $4,000 for a local charity. The Red Party fizzled out after the COVID pandemic in 2020. Also, some years ago, the employees of Wood Enterprises began a fund with voluntary payroll deductions to help employees who fell on hard times. Since its inception, the Have a Heart Fund has dispensed thousands of dollars to employees for various emergency expenses. Former employees are quick to point out the Red Party and the Have a Heart fund were started by employees and that Wood had nothing to do with them. Café Lafitte also participates in other community charity events, such as the annual Mascara Race, benefiting the New Orleans Center for Creative Arts (NOCCA). During the race, participants stop at several bars to consume a shot and put on an article of women's clothing.

EXPANDING THE EMPIRE

From the 1960s to the early 2000s, Café Lafitte in Exile maintained its reputation as a traditional cruise bar and essentially retained its gritty sensibility as the gay scene in the French Quarter underwent significant changes. Wood contributed to those changes.

In the 1980s, Wood began expanding his business empire. In 1984, he acquired the Clover Grill, across the street from Café Lafitte in Exile, from Arthur Jacobs, who opened the classic greasy spoon diner in 1945 and operated it until he retired in 1983. Jacobs had a colorful life. He was the co-owner of the Checker Cab Company and founder of the short-lived Chain Cab Company. He also served as a police officer for twenty-five years. In 1956, he was shot in the shoulder by an armed robber who tried to burglarize the restaurant. Jacobs wrestled with the thief after being shot, but the man fled the scene. Cecil Burgess was later apprehended and sentenced to fifteen years in prison. Jacobs also became a successful builder and renovator and served as executive vice president of Home Finders International, a real estate and construction company. He ran for mayor in 1984. Wood developed a friendship with Jacobs's daughter Darlene. In 2024, he bought the building housing the Clover Grill from her.

In 1984, Wood opened the notorious Rawhide, which had previously been Play It Again Sam, the Tiger Lounge, and a Black gay bar located at the intersection of St. Ann and Burgundy Streets. Rawhide quickly became known as a leather cruise bar and is immensely popular during Mardi Gras and Southern Decadence. In 1988, Wood sold the Refuge to Jerry Menefee and opened Good Friends, previously the Louisiana Purchase, at the intersection of St. Ann and Dauphine Streets. The Mystic Krewe of Barkus, which produces the annual dog parade, was born at Good Friends and remains one of the most popular Carnival parades.

And in 1992, Wood opened Poppy's Grill, which was essentially the Clover Grill with beer. Open twenty-four hours, Poppy's became something of an institution in the eight years it was open. Located at 727 St. Peter Street, the diner used "a power drill to transform a whole spud into a single spiraling potato chip several feet long." During the annual Barkus parade during Carnival season, Poppy's would host a reviewing stand, often featuring local celebrities such as Becky Allen, Angela Hill, and Margaret Orr. Wood named the place after his lover at the time, Poppy.

Wood also owns Mary's Ace Hardware on N. Rampart and other property in the French Quarter, including the often photographed "LaBranche" home at the corner of Royal and St. Peter Streets and a house on St. Ann Street. He also has business interests in Mississippi and Nevada.

The Wood empire would have tremendous success in the last quarter of the twentieth century. But that would begin to change in 2005.

5

The Shifting Role of the Gay Bar

KATRINA

The story goes that when Hurricane Katrina approached the Louisiana coast and businesses in New Orleans began to lock up and shutter their windows, something of a crisis occurred at Café Lafitte in Exile—no one knew how to lock the doors because the bar had been open twenty-four hours a day for as long as anyone could remember. But the staff figured it out, and for the first time in decades, the bar closed temporarily. Most bars in the Quarter closed, but not all of them. Katrina would mark a turning point not only in the city's history but also in the history of Café Lafitte in Exile. Although the storm did not destroy the building, it did come at a time when the role of gay bars across the nation was shifting, and Café Lafitte in Exile was no exception.

In the days after Katrina, a few doors down from the bar at the *Ambush* headquarters, Rip and Marsh Naquin Delain hosted a gathering of friends, including Michael Sullivan; Phyllis Denmark and her partner, Andy; Jay and Jay, who lived across the street; and another couple. Sullivan remembers walking the neighborhood the afternoon the storm made landfall and, unaware that the rest of the city had flooded, thinking it wasn't that bad. Two days later, they all left town.

As Katrina made landfall in the early morning hours of Monday, August 29, 2005, Javier Sandoval, a fixture in the Quarter and the gay community since 1973, and about twenty others hunkered down at Starlight by the Park on North

Rampart. None of them could have known the horrors about to befall New Orleans, but they started to get an idea when the wooden facade of the building was ripped away by the roaring winds. As the apocalypse unfolded over the next ten days, Sandoval emerged as an organizer and a leader. He recalled:

> The day after Katrina was just beautiful, not a cloud in the sky. We met at Starlight, and no one had a clue what was going on. Several queens were planning to go to the Superdome, but I talked them out of it. They would have never survived. The National Guard didn't arrive for four or five days, and when they did, they were outnumbered. It was all very Wild West, everyone fending for themselves. Some people were trying to steal money, but that was pointless because money was worthless. Cigarettes were in high demand. I owned an apartment building on Dauphine at the time. Most of my tenants left. It became a sort of compound. We had gas, so I opened a sort of soup kitchen. We also cooked and gave out water at Starlight, which was open during the day but closed up at night. Us and Johnny White's were the only bars to stay open through the whole thing.
>
> One image I'll never forget is a man leading a group of people on the neutral ground walking from the Ninth Ward to the Superdome. He had a baby in one arm and was holding another kid's hand, and behind him was a group of people that looked like a bunch of zombies. We offered them bottled water, and the look in his eyes was just so bleak. I'll never forget that.
>
> On day six, the flies became a real problem. There was obviously no garbage collection, and the flies got really bad. We made homemade flyswatters out of wire hangers, masking tape, and window screen netting. We all had duties. Each person became responsible for something. We had to ration everything. We decided to wash our hair every four days with water from the hot water heater. Somehow, around day seven, someone produced two cups of ice we rationed out among us. That was a treat.
>
> Two elderly ladies who lived across the street had stayed, and I was concerned about them. A lot of older folks who stayed were running out of medication. Someone in the nursing home by the dog park must have money or pull or something because a bus came to get them with a state police escort. I stopped the driver to ask if he would take the two sisters,

> but they didn't want to go. The trooper told me he would pretend his car had stalled and said I had twenty minutes to convince them to leave. They finally agreed and ended up leaving. That was on day five.
>
> Some have said Southern Decadence was canceled, but it wasn't. On Sunday, about thirty of us gathered at the Golden Lantern, not including the media. There was a lot of media. We marched to Johnny White's, then we went to the compound to barbecue. Thank God for booze.
>
> A lot of people we knew who smoked left their weed behind. A dealer in particular. They weren't coming back any time soon, and we needed it. So, we helped ourselves to it. It was like a rebate for years of loyalty. I finally left on day ten. My mom called from Texas and told me I needed to come home. The city was on lockdown, and nobody could get in, so I had to get to the Orleans-Jefferson line to be picked up. The whole experience was surreal. Everything you learn in the Boy Scouts about survival really came in handy. If I had to do it over again, I still would have stayed. I have no regrets. Life is too short for regrets.[1]

The weeks and months after the storm were horrific for those who stayed. Heath, a sex worker who was living in Bywater at the time, remembers going out every few days in search of food and supplies. At a store on St. Claude Avenue, he recalls police cracking open the ATM and stuffing the cash in their pockets and then announcing to the crowd they should "take what you need. There will be no food in New Orleans for a while."[2] About a month into the disaster, the National Guard knocked on Heath's door and asked him if he needed medical attention. Heath pointed out a cut in his leg he had acquired while foraging for food in a destroyed store. Over his protests, the National Guard took him to the airport, where he was told his injury would be treated. Instead, he waited in limbo for three days before he and about sixty others were put on a plane and sent to Tennessee. After three weeks there, Heath returned to New Orleans.

About a month after the storm, Lafitte's opened on a Wednesday. A large number of people attended the reopening. Two local entertainers, Tittie Toulouse and Lisa Beaumann, suggested the bar host a fundraiser for storm victims. The show was put together quickly and was scheduled for Friday. It was well attended at first, but then the Bourbon Pub a block away opened that night, and nearly everyone left to go there. Lafitte's countered by giving away free drinks, a decision that lured the crowd back. By the end of the night, the bar had raised $1,750 for Katrina relief.

After the storm, tourism fell off a great deal, which affected business at the bar, and many locals who had been regulars never returned. Some tried but said the memories of the flood were too fresh. Gradually, traditional weekly events resumed: Trash Disco on Sunday, Monday Movie Night, and Wednesday night karaoke. Despite the semi-return to normalcy, the storm's casualties and scars remained. One such loss in the queer community was Rosemary "Mama" Pino, who owned and operated five bars during the 1970s and 1980s. The beloved community leader was eighty-three years old. She died of undetermined causes in a nursing home that was not evacuated in advance of the storm. Community organizations were also damaged. Activists and other personnel were scattered across the country. Facilities and equipment were destroyed. With the city's economy shattered, the financial ability of supporters to rebuild the infrastructure of the community was also severely diminished. The political action group LAGPAC, which had made an incredible difference over the previous twenty-five years, for example, never resurfaced after Katrina.

Perhaps the most significant untold story of Katrina and its aftermath is how the queer community essentially kick-started the French Quarter after the storm. Most, if not all, of the gay bars and businesses were up and running within four weeks of the flood, and many in the LGBT+ community stayed during the whole ordeal. A month after the storm, *The Advocate* ran a cover story highlighting the effects of the flood on gay New Orleans. The edition featured several short articles, including an optimistic piece by columnist Christopher Rice, and a feature story about two lesbians determined to return to the city and rebuild. John Gotthelf stayed nearly a week before evacuating to Alabama and remembered:

> Fortunately, I had lots of cigarettes, valium, and peanut butter. I was new in town and didn't really know what was going on. I had visited New Orleans before many times as a tourist, but this was different. There was

no running water, and I stunk really bad. I was gone for four weeks and came back as soon as I learned my block had power. Returning was surreal. It was mostly deserted and looked like a third world country. Trash was everywhere. Looking back, I probably returned too soon. But a few of the gay bars were open, and that helped.[3]

PERIOD OF TRANSITION

Café Lafitte in Exile served as a refuge and reference point for gay men in the last third of the twentieth century, but that role began to change in the first quarter of the twenty-first century. Today many old-timers lament the fact that "Lafitte's aint what it used to be" and point to the mainstream acceptance of queerness as a primary reason for the erosion of traditionally gay male bars. Citing scholars Wayne Brekhus and Steven Seidman, Jaime Hartless has correctly pointed out that queer people "no longer feel forced to choose between hiding in the closet or joining a queer enclave, preferring to understand their LGBTQ identities as visible yet inconsequential parts of their selves."[4]

Indeed, the number of straight people, especially women, frequenting the bar has increased exponentially in recent years. This trend has been facilitated by Lafitte's location on Bourbon Street. Straight revelers wandering up and down the neon strip are far more likely now than in years past to cross the "lavender line" a block away and meander into the bar. Many hapless tourists looking for Lafitte's Blacksmith Shop wander into Café Lafitte in Exile, unaware they are not in the bar they are looking for. The advent of apps such as Grindr has also certainly played a role in the bar's declining gay patronage. Simply stated, gay men no longer need to go to the gay bar to find sexual partners.

While the aforementioned factors have changed the nature of gay bars nationwide, there are other, more specific reasons why Lafitte's has lost a lot of its former regulars. These reasons include the departure of longtime fixtures at the bar and a scandal that confirmed everyone's worst impressions of Tom Wood.

Former Wood Enterprises general manager Ken Grand Pre arrived in New Orleans in 1992 and began bartending at Good Friends, which Wood opened in 1988. Grand Pre became the manager of Good Friends in 1995 and was promoted to general manager of Wood Enterprises in 2001, a position he held until 2013. Grand Pre was replaced with Ken Hicks, who only stayed in the position a few months. Wood had known Hicks from Las Vegas, where Hicks was working as the manager of a building in which Wood owns a condominium. Before Grand Pre's departure, Wood had brought in another person from Las Vegas, Michael Printy, to be in charge of maintenance at Wood's properties. Printy had been the concierge at the building Hicks managed.

Hicks and Printy's short tenure at Wood Enterprises became known as the "Vegas administration." It was during this time that Wood embarked upon an ill-fated renovation of the upstairs bar at Café Lafitte in Exile. The idea was to transform the second floor into an upscale craft cocktail and wine bar. But what worked on the Vegas Strip did not travel well to Bourbon Street. The renovation landed like a lead balloon. Not only did regular patrons not like the change in atmosphere; they resented the fact that the pool table and the iconic wall mural had been removed. The upscale vibe, and the Vegas administration, did not last long.

In addition to the departure of Ken Grand Pre and changes upstairs, other factors contributed to the loss of patronage at the bar. In 2017, Café Lafitte in Exile lost two of its most loyal patrons—Rip and Marsha Naquin-Delain, founders and publishers of *Ambush Magazine,* who lived less than a half-block from the bar. The old "Ambush Mansion" in the 800 block of Bourbon Street had been their home since the mid-1980s and also served as *Ambush* headquarters. In their thirty-plus-year tenure as the magazine's publishers, Naquin and Delain became fixtures in the French Quarter's queer community. In addition to founding the magazine, they also founded the Krewe of Queenateenas (which names a King Cake Queen each Carnival season), they produced the annual Gay Appreciation Awards and the annual Gay Easter Parade, and tirelessly promoted Southern Decadence, of which they served as grand marshals in 2015. They were tireless fundraisers for local charities and generally regarded as larger-than-life figures.

Rip and Marsha, as they were universally known, were an enigmatic couple—mysterious and intriguing yet aloof and unapproachable. There was something about them that made people want to know them. Rip, gregarious, boisterous, and magnetic, the gravity of his charisma drawing people to him. And Marsha,

Rip and Marsha Naquin-Delain, ca. 2015. Courtesy of *Ambush Magazine.*

calm and quiet, surrounding Rip like a forcefield keeping callers at a safe distance. Together, they were a bright star in the gay French Quarter galaxy.

Rip grew up in rural South Louisiana and attended college at Nicholls University in Thibodeaux, about an hour from New Orleans. Sometimes, on weekends, Rip and his fraternity brothers would go to New Orleans to party. On these occasions, Rip would usually find a reason to break away from the pack and go to the gay bars on the far end of Bourbon Street. When it was discovered that Rip was gay, his fraternity chapter called a meeting and voted to expel him. Traumatized, he quit school and came out to his father, who told him, "You're gonna end up like those queers in New Orleans who burned"—a reference to the Up Stairs Lounge fire, which had recently happened. The first time Rip brought Marsha (Marty) home, his dad told him, "Don't you ever bring him home again!" Rip's reaction? "I didn't speak to my family for ten years." Marsha's coming out was less painful. Marsha grew up in Baton Rouge and came out to her mom when she was fifteen. Mom, a police officer, was incredibly supportive, but they agreed it was best not to tell Dad, a local high school football coach. Marsha's mother used to drop him off at the gay bars so he could explore "the lifestyle" and even introduced him to her hairstylist, who became Marsha's first boyfriend.

Rip and Marsha's was a love story for the ages. They remained together until their deaths in 2017. After Rip died, in August, Marsha sold *Ambush* to Tomy Acosta, who still publishes it today. Café Lafitte in Exile, which had for decades advertised in the magazine (for many years, the bar had the coveted back cover), decided to pull their ads after Acosta took over the paper. Had Rip and Marsha not passed away in 2017 (Marsha died that December), they would have faced a dilemma the following year: specifically, the decision to cover and publish the story of a brewing scandal involving Wood, a loyal advertiser in *Ambush* for years.

SCANDAL

In 2018, Wood Enterprises was confronted with a scandal that would have long-term consequences. It involved Wood directly and centered on one of the three bars he owned in the French Quarter—the building at 740 Burgundy Street, which had been a gay bar long before Tom Wood opened Rawhide. Rawhide was a leather bar with a masculine aesthetic and soon earned a reputation as a notorious cruise bar because of its dimly lit back pool table area and adjacent bathrooms. In these areas, cruising was common, and anonymous sexual encounters were de rigueur. The only other gay leather bar in New Orleans that had a "dark room" was the Phoenix. Like Rawhide, this bar was also known for its sexual activity. In late 2018, both bars were investigated and cited by the Louisiana Office of Alcohol and Tobacco Control (ATC). Many in the bar scene and leather community believed the state crackdown on both bars was motivated by homophobia, but this was not the case. Rather, the crackdowns originated within the queer community and resulted from vengeance.

On September 6, 2018, someone filed a complaint against Rawhide with the New Orleans Police Department, which in turn referred the complaint to the ATC. The complaint read as follows: "This establishment allows lewd public sex acts, including oral, anal, group sex, and masturbation in clear view of patrons. There is also a room in the back of the bar in which people engage in obscene and lewd sex acts. Male prostitutes solicit (including those that may be minors). Drugs are rampant. Wed. Fri. and Sat. after 9 pm are best times to view."

Within the ATC, the complaint was referred to the Human Trafficking Task Force. The ATC then launched an investigation, which included a compliance check as well as an undercover investigation. Two undercover agents were then sent into Rawhide on four separate occasions and witnessed (and surreptitiously recorded with hidden cameras) multiple sex acts (including oral, anal, and masturbation), hardcore gay pornography on multiple television sets, pup play, and popper use. After receiving the undercover agents' reports, ATC commissioner Juana Lombard offered a settlement agreement to Tom Wood, who declined the offer. Wood wanted to contest the charges, despite the overwhelming abundance of evidence.

An administrative hearing was then held, which lasted roughly four and a half hours and featured surreptitiously recorded video footage of sex acts as well as attempts to explain away the pornography as "art films"; further, Wood Enterprises claimed that management had no idea sex acts were occurring on the premises.[5] Commissioners questioned why there was a large sign forbidding cell phone use in the back room but not in the front bar. They also questioned why there was no sign on the door of what the defense claimed was an ADA (Americans with Disabilities Act) bathroom indicating it as such. The defense argued that nudity is not to be unexpected in a bathroom and that bathrooms inherently assume an "expectation of privacy." But Commissioner Lombard was having none of it, calling the defense arguments "disingenuous" and citing a culture that fostered sexual activity.

At the conclusion of the hearing, Rawhide was cited with twelve violations—eight counts of pornography on the televisions and four counts of sexual activity on the premises—and fined $6,750. The bar was also cited for serving a minor. The bar's license was suspended for thirty days, with three of those weeks being deferred. In other words, the bar had to close for one week. A sixty-day probation period was also imposed.

At the time, there was widespread speculation about who had filed the complaint against Rawhide. That person has never been publicly identified. However, based on what is known, one can make a reasonable assumption of who it was. An investigative report published in *Ambush* states:

> The complaint against Rawhide was filed on September 6, 2018, a few days after Southern Decadence. On Sunday of Southern Decadence weekend (September 2), after the parade, three women attempted to enter Rawhide to attend an event (a leather and kink demonstration) being sponsored by the Crescent City Leathermen and were turned away, one of whom became very angry when they were not allowed into the bar. The security personnel then called Michael Musa, the General Manager of Wood Enterprises, who spoke to the agitated woman. Again, she was denied entry . . . The previous night—actually early Sunday morning—another woman who was denied entry at Rawhide began screaming and causing a minor scene, which was witnessed by several people, one of whom heard the woman shout, "I will call and have this place shut down."
>
> What is unclear is why the complainant did not report gender discrimination. Whoever the complainant was possessed knowledge of the activities that regularly occurred in the back room and suggests the complainant had visited the bar before.
>
> It's safe to assume the complainant was acting out of spite because the crux of the complaint (underage prostitution) was false and ultimately dismissed by the ATC. At the same time, it is understandable why the complainant was angry. Louisiana law (statute 51:2247) prohibits discrimination in public accommodations based on sex or gender. Some have speculated the complainant was not even in New Orleans at the time of the incident and was reacting to the incident after reading about it on social media.
>
> Whatever the case, the fact remains—refusing a woman entry to a bar just because she is a woman is unconstitutional and illegal . . . The complaint may also have come from the other woman who was denied entry the night before and who threated to "have this place shut down."[6]

During the ATC's administrative hearing against Wood Enterprises, it was revealed that Tom Wood had filed a complaint against the Phoenix (a competing bar with a similar reputation) in response to the charges Rawhide was facing. A redacted copy of the complaint letter provided by ATC dated December 4, 2018, requesting an investigation of the Phoenix reads as follows:

Rawhide, 2010. Collins C. Diboll Vieux Carré Digital Survey, The Historic New Orleans Collection, 2_087_burg_736-740.

[letterhead redacted]

Dear Commissioner Lombard and Linda:

I am writing to request that a confidential investigation be conducted concerning the operations of The Phoenix Bar. Based upon information and belief, lewd and improper conduct occurs on a regular basis within the licensed premises in violation of La. R.S. 26:90 (A)(13) and (D)(1). Particularly, the upstairs bar, known as "The Eagle," is an environment where there is little illumination and sexual acts are taking place within the view of other patrons and staff and in the bathrooms . . . Additionally, pornographic videos are played for public viewing in violation of La. R.S. 26:90(G)(1). On Fridays, they offer "all you can drink" draft beer from 9 pm–midnight in violation of La. R.S. 26:90(A)(15). [redacted] and its customers have started frequenting its main competitor, The Phoenix Bar. I ask that this investigation take place so that all "leather" bars operate within the same parameters.

If you have any questions concerning the foregoing, please do not hesitate to contact me.

Very truly yours,
[name and signature redacted][7]

Undercover investigative visits to the Phoenix conducted by ATC witnessed and recorded multiple sex acts in the bar and several instances of pornography being shown on the televisions. In light of the video evidence, the owners of the Phoenix did not contest these citations.

According to Phoenix owner Clint Taylor, after the initial complaint against the Phoenix was filed on December 4, a slew of other complaints against the bar were filed with a variety of government agencies at both the state and local levels. According to the investigative report in *Ambush:*

On December 30, New Orleans Police showed up at the Phoenix after receiving a call from a customer who claimed to be "appalled" that the bar was showing pornography. The officers were surprised to see not porn but rather the Saints-Panthers game being shown. The police figured it was a crank call and no action was taken.

On February 15, the State Fire Marshal's office showed up at the Phoenix and said someone had called them and reported fearing for his life because there was no emergency exit upstairs. Taylor pointed out the drop-down fire escape. Fire officials noted that the escape was not up to code and told him to close the upstairs bar. Taylor pointed out the age and layout of the building made it virtually impossible to bring the escape up to code. Fire officials agreed and informed him they would look into the matter. Four days later on February 19, they returned and allowed Taylor he could reopen the upstairs bar. When Taylor asked who made the complaint, State Fire Marshal officials told him they could not reveal that information.

On the same day, February 19, as the State Fire Marshal officials were leaving, Louisiana State Police Video Gaming enforcement officials showed up at the Phoenix in response to a complaint that the bar did not have a "No Minors Allowed" sign posted. Apparently, someone had removed the sign which was posted on the door to the bar. The officer told Taylor he had remembered the sign was posted during a recent routine inspection and told him to put up another one. No official action was taken.

On February 21, ATC issued the Phoenix a summons stating [Taylor] was in violation of a state law that says "Beer Busts" cannot continue after 10:00 pm. Taylor regularly donates kegs for beer busts sponsored by various bear, leather, and athletic organizations.

On February 22, the New Orleans Fire Department showed up at the Phoenix in response to a call from a concerned citizen claiming there were no fire extinguishers at the bar. Fire Department officials left somewhat frustrated after Taylor pointed out all the fire extinguishers in the bar. No action was taken.

On February 26, the office of Building and Permits showed up at the Phoenix in response to reports of smoking being allowed in the bar. This complaint was in addition to a similar accusation in the December 4 complaint. Taylor showed the agents the enclosed smoking patio. Inspectors told him the smoking patio was legal but that he needed a larger exhaust fan. A larger exhaust fan has since been installed. No official action was taken, and smoking is currently permitted in that designated area.[8]

Although never confirmed, many people assumed these complaints originated with Wood Enterprises. In his investigative report, Perez writes:

> The proximity in time of the complaints (six in less than a month) suggests they may have originated from the same source. In addition, the nature of the complaints suggest they came from someone familiar with state and local laws governing bars. A source close to the investigation confirms that at least one of the complaints came from a rival bar owner. During the course of one of several interviews with Taylor, Taylor recounted a long history of complaints from a nearby rival bar owner. Many in the community assumed the repeated complaints came from Tom Wood since he admitted in the Administrative Hearing that he had filed the initial complaint against the Phoenix.[9]

When asked for comment, an attorney for Wood Enterprises issued the following statement: "When Mr. Wood realized that the ATC's unequal treatment was giving more favorable treatment to a competing business, such as the Phoenix, resulting in a loss of business to Rawhide, Mr. Wood cried 'Foul!' Wood Enterprises . . . made purely a business decision to insure that all establishments in the City of New Orleans were on an equal footing and not receiving more favorable treatment than other similarly situated businesses."

While it is true that the punitive measures taken against Rawhide were more severe than those taken against the Phoenix, it is important to note that Wood's attorney issued the aforementioned statement before the Phoenix penalties were announced. The more likely explanation for the difference in penalties is the fact that the Phoenix accepted a settlement agreement, whereas Rawhide did not.

When both bars were cited, the sexual activity for which they were known ceased. This caused great distress within the leather community. Notably, people were angry not about the gender discrimination but, rather, at Wood for turning in the Phoenix. Many people viewed this as a betrayal, and they blamed Wood for the loss of "safe gay spaces." In the minds of many, the ordeal reinforced the already established image of Wood as a supremely selfish and greedy businessman who had no sense of loyalty or commitment to the community. Some longtime employees of Rawhide quit in protest. Others quit because business had taken a turn for the worse. A few people argued Wood was only doing what any shrewd businessman would do, but these voices were the minority. A boycott of all Wood Enterprises businesses in New Orleans ensued—its slogan "Stay Out of the Woods." The boycott affected the bars but not significantly. Nevertheless, Wood Enterprises responded with a short-lived and ineffective public relations campaign emphasizing they "Welcomed Everyone."

Business at Rawhide began to suffer, not so much because of the boycott but because the nature of the bar had changed. The notorious back room no longer hosted the action that had in previous decades made it so infamous. Regular patronage fell off, and more and more women started showing up at the bar. To the shock and dismay of many, there were even sightings of bachelorette parties there. Rawhide limped along for a few years until Wood decided to rename and rebrand the bar. Wood dubbed the new incarnation "the Silver Fox." But the Silver Fox was a dud, and in 2023, Wood changed the name back to Rawhide.

Around the time of the Rawhide-Phoenix scandal, business at Café Lafitte had already begun to decline. Ten years earlier, Lafitte's was still essentially a gay bar, but in recent years, straight patronage at the bar has increased significantly. This had much to do with its location. Because of the pedestrian tourist flow on Bourbon Street, more and more straight people frequent the bar, many mistakenly assuming they are at Lafitte's Blacksmith Shop. In years past, the heavy gay crowd, inside and outside the bar, alerted clueless straight tourists they were not at the Lafitte's they were looking for. But with the regular gay patronage gone, there was nothing to alert the hapless pirate seekers. This is especially evident on Sunday afternoons. For years, Trash Disco attracted a large crowd to the bar. By late afternoon or early evening, the bar would be packed with gay men enjoying the retro music in anticipation of the "napkin toss." As the playlist got closer to John Paul Young's "Love Is in the Air," the bar was so packed that the crowd overflowed into the street. In recent years, the napkin toss crowd has shifted to the Bourbon Pub, and finding a seat at the bar at Lafitte's is no trouble at all. These changes have sharpened since the COVID pandemic of 2020.

PANDEMIC AND PRIDE

The effects of the COVID-19 outbreak in New Orleans were profound. In March 2020, the state and city governments effectively shut the city down, and commerce came to a screeching halt. And the timing could not have been worse—it was the peak of the tourist season. The gig economy evaporated overnight, and service industry workers were among the worst affected. At the time, Rhodes Murphy wrote, "With most of the city's tourism and hospitality workforce—the largest source of employment in New Orleans—out of a job, the city is quickly becoming a case study for how a frayed social safety net responds in a global pandemic."[10]

For months, bars in the French Quarter had to navigate an ever-changing set of rules and regulations issued from City Hall. First the bars were closed completely, then they could open but only serve drinks to go, then there were no to-go drinks, then they could accommodate indoor guests but at a limited capacity. And there were curfews as well. Bartenders struggled not only to make money but also to enforce mask mandates and social distancing guidelines, which many tourists from "red states" utterly disregarded. Through it all, many regular bar patrons chose to just stay home.

During the COVID shutdown, some bars closed for good, including the legendary, original Johnny White's, a longtime fixture on St. Peter Street. When the owner of the building housing Betty's Bar & Bistro refused to work with bar owner Tomy Acosta on the rent, Acosta closed the bar and told the landlord he was moving out. The landlord quickly had a change of heart and renegotiated the lease. Betty's survived COVID but could not survive the post-COVID decline in business and closed for good in 2023. Other bar (and business) owners in the French Quarter have struggled to reach pre-COVID levels.

It was during the COVID-19 pandemic that another significant development in the history of Wood Enterprises occurred—its takeover of New Orleans Pride. In 2020, New Orleans Pride imploded, and Tom Wood picked up the pieces.

With such a large gay population as well as its love of parades, one would think New Orleans would host a vibrant Pride celebration each June, but such has never been the case. In attempting to explain why, many people point to the weather. June in New Orleans is simply unbearable. The heat and humidity are oppressive, and almost daily afternoon showers don't help. To a lesser extent, the popularity of Southern Decadence, held over the Labor Day weekend, may also explain why Pride in New Orleans has never lived up to its full potential.

Since the late 1970s, when the first Gay Fest was organized, Pride in New Orleans has been organized by a variety of different groups. From 2011 to 2020, it was under the auspices of New Orleans Pride, which was led by Chris Leonard. During his tenure, Leonard did an excellent job of organizing and growing the annual parade. The parade was canceled in 2020 because of the pandemic, but as the parade date approached, Leonard made a post on social media asking how people were going to celebrate Pride since there would be no parade. The post concluded with a request that people refrain from including political content in their comments. This request struck many as bizarre, considering Pride is essentially political in nature. A controversy ensued and exposed a tangle of nerves that had long surrounded New Orleans Pride—specifically, that it was dominated by privileged white cisgender gay men. There was some truth to the allegation, a fact evidenced by the existence of lesser-known New Orleans Pride organizations such as Black Pride. Amid the subsequent firestorm his post created, Leonard shifted blame to his board of directors, some of whom resigned in protest. Leonard then resigned, and New Orleans Pride as an organization was dissolved. Enter Tom Wood. In 2021, Wood Enterprises assumed control and began organizing the annual parade. Those in the community familiar with Wood's reputation noted the irony of him taking over an event recently destroyed by white cis privilege, but the incongruity of having a Trump supporter organizing a Pride parade was lost on most. Many of the parade participants are probably not aware of Wood's politics or his history.

Nevertheless, various groups have staged protests during the parade in an attempt to raise awareness about Wood and his politics. In 2024, during the war between Israel and Gaza, pro-Palestinian protesters disrupted the NOLA Pride Parade. A coalition of nine advocacy groups called the "People's Coalition for Palestine" conducted a protest rally at the steps fronting Jackson Square just before the parade started. About one hundred people attended the rally, which featured speakers from each of the coalition organizations—Queer and Trans Community Action Project (QTCAP), Renters Rights Assembly, Tulane and Loyola Students for a Democratic Society, Sunrise Movement New Orleans, Jewish Voice for Peace, New Orleans Stop Helping Israel's Ports, Krewe of Chickpea, and NOLA Musicians for Palestine. Protesters held signs that read, "No Pride in Genocide," "Down with Corporate Pride," "Cops Don't Belong at Pride," and "Fuck Shell & Bayer."

As the parade inched its way down Decatur Street, several protesters interrupted the parade and caused it to stop for about fifteen minutes as they staged a "die-in" to raise awareness about the NOLA Pride Parade's corporate sponsors' support for Israel's war in Gaza. In an unrelated article about Northshore Pride by Lucas Harrell, Blu DiMarco, a member of QTCAP, said, "Corporations don't care about queer identity or culture, instead they use us, and pride parades, as a means for profit."[11]

Objecting in general to the parade's corporate sponsorship, the coalition specifically targeted Shell and Bayer as well as Wood Enterprises. Protesters cited the State of Israel's purchase of 260 thousand tons of crude oil from Shell to fuel its war effort and a pesticide Bayer manufactures and sells to Israel, which uses it to render Palestinian land unsuitable for agriculture. They also called out Wood Enterprises for its history of racism, misogyny, and transphobia. Participants in the die-in left when the New Orleans Police Department issued a dispersal order, and no one was arrested. Organizer Willem Myers noted, "We created enough agitation for it to be meaningful, but not dangerous for those involved."[12] Spectator reaction was mixed and ranged from confusion, amusement, anger, and bewilderment. Myers believed that initially many people probably assumed they were far-right Christian fundamentalists—another group that regularly protests queer events.

CHAMELEON SYNDROME

Hurricane Katrina, the Rawhide-Phoenix scandal, and the pandemic coincided with changing times. At the dawn of the new millennium, public attitudes regarding queerness were changing, and with those changes, the role of gay bars was changing too. With the rise of the internet, smartphones, and dating apps, the gay bar became decentered as the crux of gay life.

Back in the decades when most closet doors were firmly shut and long before the internet became a thing, the role of the gay bar was monumental in the lives of gay men. It is difficult for young people to imagine a world with no social or sex networking sites, no gay characters on television (or gay-themed television shows, for that matter), no cars with rainbow stickers. The threat of being arrested merely for being gay is utterly incomprehensible to them. They never knew a world in which queerness was invisible. But that world did exist. It was a world of darkness for gay men, a world where their core beings were hidden. It was a world of pretense, of false realities and double lives. In such a world, the gay bar afforded these men the only opportunity to be themselves, to let the light shine, if only for a few hours, on their true identities.

Identity in general is a complicated thing—for the gay man doubly so, and for the closeted, even more complex still. We all assume various and sometimes competing identities: son, father, husband, employee, coworker, friend. For the straight man, negotiating the tensions that accompany multiple identities is manageable because his external world is permeated with examples and reference points. But for a young gay man who doesn't know what the word *gay* means, an adolescent who lives in a society where homosexuality doesn't exist except in clinical psychiatric textbooks on mental disorders and in hushed whispers at family reunions and vitriolic sermons on eternal damnation—what reference point does he have? The gay bar, of course.

The gay bar for decades served not only as refuge and playground for gay men who had grown comfortable in their roles as would-be outcast sodomites but also as identity giver for those just coming to terms with their queerness. Dudley Clendinen and Adam Nagourney describe gay bars before gay visibility this way: "If bars in the '60s still symbolized the rights of manhood to traditional young males, to young gay males trying to find the missing context of their lives, what a gay bar promised was much more: freedom, shelter, friendship, excitement, romance, seduction—escape." For young and old alike, the gay bar was a safe space and a place for answers for those who felt the burgeoning yearnings of the identity that dare not speak its name.

"Charlie Bear," a regular at Café Lafitte for forty-six years, grew up in a large family on Esplanade Avenue. His parents, who were forward-thinking, would take Charlie and his nine siblings, when they were children, walking along Bourbon Street and point out the strip clubs and the gay bars and other adult venues they would face soon enough. Charlie first went to Café Lafitte in Exile in 1964, at the age of fifteen. At that time, the DJ booth didn't exist, and that space was known as the "blow job corner." There Charlie received his first blow job by three older men he guesses must have been in their late twenties or thirty-something. A few years later, Charlie fought in Vietnam, came home, married a woman, and had children. Charlie eventually divorced his wife and came out to his children. A fixture at the bar, he credited Café Lafitte in Exile with helping him become comfortable with his sexuality.

Other men convey the same sentiment: that Café Lafitte provided them a reference point of what it meant to be gay. This feeling is true for young and old alike, who span the decades from the bar's inception to its current scene. Consider the story of Mike. Mike grew up in a small town in Pennsylvania where there was only one gay bar, which patrons had to enter through a back alley. When he came out to his brother, his brother's response was, "Move to New Orleans and never talk to me again." Not long afterward, Mike's job as a traveling nurse brought him to New Orleans. Like so many visitors, he fell in love with New Orleans and never left. Mike reports being shocked at how easy it was to be gay in New Orleans when he arrived in 1997, but he was still fearful of discrimination and homophobia. He began making the rounds along "the fruit loop." He describes Café Lafitte this way: "This bar is different because it's more relaxed, comfortable. No one feels the need to pretend to be someone they're not. Lafitte's is my gay Cheers. Lafitte's helped me decide who I didn't want to be and molded who I became. Lafitte's is like New Orleans itself—always a character around, someone to talk to, always something to learn."[13]

One thing Charlie Bear and Mike and countless others have learned is that being gay in a homophobic society means embracing the chameleon syndrome, that is, assuming a variety of identities that adapt according to circumstance and evolve over time. Indeed, time itself is a chameleon, constantly shuffling perspectives like the multiple facets of the prism through which identity is viewed. Identity, and the cluster of meanings associated with it, is a gradually unfolding, multilayered onion riddle whose ultimate resolution comes with time.

John Gotthelf, a retired high school counselor, offered this meditation on the subject of identity:

> I was more gay when I first came out than I am now. Being gay is just a small part of who I am. I grew up in Yazoo City, a small town in the Mississippi Delta. My parents didn't even tell me I was Jewish until I was twelve or thirteen because the Klan was very active there at that time. And I didn't come to terms with my sexuality until I was thirty-one. I had been in therapy for about a year, and during one session, my psychiatrist simply told me, "You're gay," and it made sense. Growing up, I had no exposure to gay people. Coming out was scary but fun.[14]

If anything, Café Lafitte over the decades has (in addition to providing a place for gay men to get laid) provided a safe space, a refuge, if you will, from the chameleon syndrome. But the sanctuary of the gay bar may have had a negative consequence as well. Because gay bars afforded gay men one of the few opportunities to explore their sexuality (usually in the form of quasi-anonymous/quasi-public sex acts) and because those "crimes" were publicly exposed in newspapers following arrests, the stereotype that gay men are more promiscuous than straight men was born. Judith Butler, one of the founding luminaries of queer theory, observes, "There is no gender identity behind the expressions of gender . . . identity is performatively constituted by the very 'expressions' that are said to be its results." Butler's claim may be debatable, but it certainly explains straight society's once prevailing view that gay men are obsessed with sex.

Many of the men we interviewed in researching this book voiced the same reason for becoming a regular at Café Lafitte: they felt comfortable because it's such a friendly place, which is somewhat amazing considering the demographic mix of people who frequent the bar. Unlike most gay bars, Café Lafitte does not cater to a particular type. This characteristic probably stems from the fact that Lafitte's was well established before gay bars began to cater to specific subgroups. On any given day or night in its "heyday," you could find at Lafitte's a couple of bears chatting amiably with a pair of twinks, who may be sitting next to a bevy of lesbians entertaining a straight couple that haplessly wandered into the bar, while a drag queen plays video poker not far away, and in the corner next to the eternal flame, an elderly gentleman tries to attract the attention of a twenty-one-year-old hustler who just sashayed in. Age, color, wealth, orientation, and scene preference are irrelevant at Lafitte's, arrogance frowned upon. Cliquish it is not.

Longtime popular at Lafitte's, DJ Myke came out in 1979 at age nineteen. Upon discovering some poppers (muscle relaxants) and a few gay magazines in his room, his mother, both sad and furious, called his father at work. Myke was asked to leave his house. Full reconciliation with his parents would take twenty years. A few years earlier, when he was seventeen, he had his first sexual experience with a man. He was working as a cashier at a store when an older man propositioned him. In 1980, he started making the rounds at the gay bars. He had been reluctant to go to the bars because of the movie *Cruising,* staring Al Pacino, which was about a serial killer targeting men in the gay leather scene. He found Café Lafitte's particularly "fearful" because it was "dark and mysterious."[15]

Longtime regular Tim Kinzel recalls:

> I started going to Lafitte's because a bartender I liked got a job there. He didn't last long, but I stuck around because I felt comfortable there. The crowd was a bit older, which was nice because at the pub, where I was hanging out before, I felt old. I preferred the upstairs bar at Lafitte's because it was easier to talk to people, the music wasn't as loud as it was downstairs, and it was usually less crowded—except on the weekends, when people cruised the pool table area. I met my one and only one-night stand at the pool table. We called the guy "Rodeo Bob" because he said he was in town for a rodeo. We went to the ladies' restroom to fool around, and then we went to my place.[16]

Every gay man sooner or later gets in touch with his inner Dorothy and has at some point his "Toto Epiphany," that moment when he realizes he's gay. Because of societal shifts in the general public's attitude regarding queerness, that realization is no longer as universally terrifying as it used to be. Many young people today come out naturally with no problems. But many do not. Homophobia and transphobia persist, a fact evidenced by depression and suicide rates among LGBT+ people and the recent wave of anti-queer legislation sweeping through Republican-controlled legislatures. For young people who have been raised in deeply religious families, coming out is often accompanied by a sense of dread and horror. Self-loathing and revulsion are only the beginning. What follows is mourning. And grieving. And sadness. And loss. Especially loss. Deep loss. Profound loss. Then, for the truly courageous, acceptance, which gradually gives way to fulfillment.

Today young people have numerous reference points of what it means to be queer—mass media, popular culture, the internet, among others. But that wasn't always the case. Frank Perez recalls his own Toto Epiphany, occurring in college with a fraternity brother, in a 2008 journal entry:

> Being out and proud was unthinkable to us then. On weekends, we would escape the closet and drive down to New Orleans from LSU. Lafitte's gave us a chance not only to be ourselves but also to catch a glimpse of the gay world. As our relationship grew, we each dealt with our gayness in radically different ways: he joined the marines and felt all the more macho for it. I became a fundamentalist Christian and felt all the less sinful for

> it. Fortunately, his macho phase and my self-righteous phase didn't last long. But while they did, he went off to war and I transferred to another school, but we did keep in touch for several years and from time to time meet in New Orleans at Lafitte's.

Perez recalls those later reunions.

> One of those occasions stands out in my memory. I had arrived in town before him and was waiting for him at the bar. I was sitting at the back point where the DJ booth now is when he came in. As soon as I saw him, I was reminded of Wordsworth's famous definition of poetry: "powerful feelings recollected in tranquility." Memories, and their accompanying emotions, began to surge. Not just the incredible, ineffable, unrepeatable euphoria of falling in love for the first time but also that untroubled spirit of youth—the dreams and hopes that lure us into young adulthood, the invincibility that reassures us we can do anything and never bothers to tell us we will one day die. How paradoxical to be so confident yet lack so much experience!
>
> The morning after that meeting, I considered all the gifts time gives us if we accept them, the most generous of which, I think, is perspective.

CHANGING TIMES

Traditional gay bars across the nation are changing. The need they once met—providing a place for queer people to meet other queer people (at least in urban areas) is rapidly diminishing. In his 2016 memoir, *The Double Life,* David Lee Campbell writes of being closeted in New Orleans in the 1950s:

> These were risky times to be gay in any city in America. In New Orleans, in the 1950s and for many years, the police, for no reason, would periodically raid the few gay bars in the Quarter (the only venues where gay people could meet and socialize), round up several patrons and bartenders, and haul them off to jail . . . to the horror of every gay person, the photographs and addresses of those arrested, not convicted of anything, were

> published in the *Times-Picayune* for all to see, destroying or seriously jeopardizing careers, breaking up families and relationships, and occasionally ending in suicide, for being in a place where one simply sought to be with one's own . . . I was terrified in many ways and most of the time.[17]

The evolution of gay bars as they adapt to larger cultural changes and shifts in public attitudes (to say nothing of technology) has become a major topic of research for queer theorists, sociologists, and anthropologists. Numerous books and multitudes of scholarly articles in academic journals have been published on the topic in the last twenty years. These scholars and their studies confirm what veteran gay bar-goers already knew from personal experience. Referring to the shifting role of gay bars, for example, sociologist Jaime Hartless has observed: "Queer spaces like the gay bar have historically served as bulwarks against heteronormativity, helping LGBTQ people build community and resist marginalization . . . However, in this increasingly tolerant climate, some theorists argue that many LGBTQ individuals are now able to live openly outside the confines of the closet . . . at least so long as they embody homonormativity by otherwise appearing 'normal' according to heterosexual mores." Hartless calls this conditional acceptance "questionable queerness." The social transformations cited by Hartless and witnessed by older gays, much to the lament of many of them, raises another question: is it wise, or even necessary, to still divide "the world into spaces that are queer and spaces that are not"?[18]

Regarding straight tourists, Hartless questions "whether what they really appreciate is how the homonormativity of these venues allows straight patrons to perform 'tolerance' without meaningfully challenging their own heteronormative sensibilities. The cumulative costs of such homonormativity may drive some LGBTQ people away from places where they should feel welcome."[19] Such behavior would certainly explain the loss of gay patronage at Café Lafitte in Exile among older gay men.

As society continues to evolve, the loss of a "binary view of heterosexual-homosexual leisure spaces" may be inevitable.[20] In the case of Café Lafitte in Exile, this trend is in some ways a throwback to the bar's earlier incarnation at 941 Bourbon Street, when its sexuality was fluid.

In 2024, Wood instructed his bartenders to stop offering discounted drink prices to locals, an unpopular move that resulted in the loss of local patronage. Longtime regulars viewed the loss of the locals' discount as a proverbial "slap in the face" and a complete surrender to the tourist trade. The vast majority of tourists who patronize Café Lafitte in Exile are straight, a fact that raises a question raised elsewhere in this book: what makes a gay bar gay?

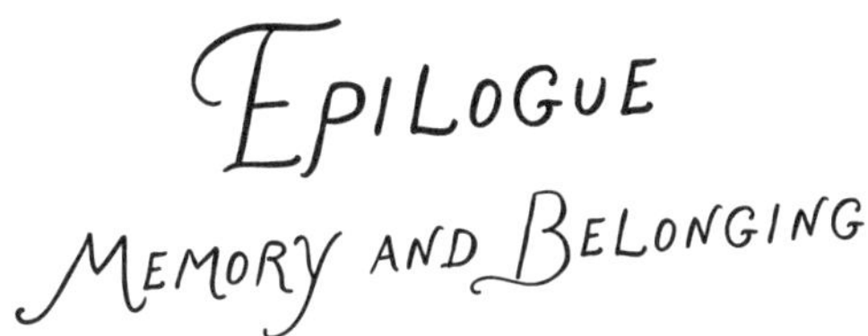

Epilogue: Memory and Belonging

THE RELIABILITY OF MEMORY

Skylar Fein's 2008 exhibit on the Up Stairs Lounge fire at the Jonathan Ferrara gallery for Prospect 1 established him as one of the city's most promising new artists. The following year, he had a solo exhibit at the New Orleans Museum of Art and another in 2010 at VOLTA New York. Fein's work has been favorably reviewed in notable publications such as *Art in America, ArtForum,* the *New York Times,* the *New Yorker,* and the *Times-Picayune,* but when he came to New Orleans in 2005, he had no artistic training whatsoever. The story of his success is a fascinating account of how New Orleans, even at its worst, is a source of artistic inspiration.

Originally from New York, Fein moved to New Orleans six weeks before Hurricane Katrina. He evacuated to Tennessee for a month and, upon returning to New Orleans, realized he needed furniture. Combing through the endless piles of rubble that littered the city, he gathered enough debris to build a table and chairs. His ingenuity impressed his friends and others, and soon he was meeting a demand for more furniture. This endeavor awakened his creativity, and then one day he was walking down Iberville Street when he noticed a plaque on the sidewalk commemorating the Up Stairs Lounge fire. Upon reading the plaque, Fein recalls thinking to himself, "How do I not know about this?"

"The seediness of the block" and "the handsomeness of the building" were "tantalizing," and thus ensued six months of research into the fire that culminated in his exhibit *Remember the Up Stairs Lounge.* That show established Fein as an up-and-coming artist, but it wasn't his first exhibit. Fein's premiere exhibition was at the notorious leather bar the Phoenix. Fein recalls:

> A casual tourist to 1950s New Orleans might have missed the seedy second-floor bookstore on Rampart Street. But in the gay subculture of the time, Henkin's Adonis, with its cruisy magazine racks, private booths and tiny movie theater, was a place notorious and beloved.
>
> When the city bulldozed the area to build a park in 1971, a treasure trove of gay history was lost.
>
> But it wasn't lost forever.
>
> In 2005, gay photographer Leonard Earl Johnson was clearing out a friend's garage just outside the Quarter—the friend was elderly and no longer had the strength to do hurricane cleanup—when he made a surprising find: a dusty old sign with a picture of a cowboy.
>
> He wiped his hand across it, and as he made out the word "Henkin," he got a shiver of recognition. He looked around the garage. It was stacked with the original signs of Henkin's Adonis—three decades of them. When he showed them to me the next day, he was still shaking with excitement.
>
> I told the manager of the local leather bar about the staggering find. She suggested an art show—right there in the bar. So, on Saturday night, in the back room of the second sleaziest bar in New Orleans, we hung the signs of Henkin's Adonis. Crowds of gay men came to pay homage to the lost Atlantis of sleaze, sex and self-acceptance.
>
> There's just one thing wrong with this story. I made it up.
>
> Henkin's Adonis never existed. I painted the signs myself, lovingly sketching believable images (cowboys, farm hands) and tag lines ("Physique and body-building")—code words that gay men in the 1950s and '60s understood. I distressed the signs, sanding and rubbing them with dirt to simulate the passing of so many years.
>
> But here's the weird part. (That was the normal part.) The men who came to the opening remembered the Adonis in every detail.

> They recounted the flirtations among the magazines, the hand-jobs in the tiny theater, the time they were arrested coming out . . . of Henkin's Adonis. I had crafted bogus newspaper articles from the Adonis' last day (never happened), when patrons famously rioted against the cops sent to clear the building (completely false), when locals held a vigil and brought flowers as the bulldozers revved up (a fantasy), and I'd blown up the clippings and hung them on the wall, too. People remembered the coverage.
>
> I would say that half the bar knew it was a lark, and the other half was absolutely convinced it was real and had the memories to prove it. If anyone asked me directly, I told the truth: it was my homage to the gay men of another time, whose fighting and loving made it possible for me to live openly today. But to the men who talked and talked without asking a question, I simply smiled and nodded along, a student of their sometimes-unsteady eldership.
>
> This probably says a lot about memory, its creation and fabrication. It may say a lot about gay men, or about New Orleans, which still provides the gutter for all America to lie in cheaply and conveniently. All I know for sure is what the Adonis sign says: "We never close."

This anecdote illustrates a central truth and raises questions about the reliability of memory. There is a lively debate among historians regarding the value of oral history.[1] In his book *Truth in History,* Oscar Handlin argues much oral history is unreliable because of the "vagaries of memory" and "the possibility of self-serving interest on the part of the speaker."[2] One of the primary challenges for people researching and documenting queer history is that so much of it remains in the closet. Until recent decades, being queer was not something people wanted to document because of the terrible costs of being outed—being jailed, fired, evicted, ostracized, institutionalized, and so on. Consequently, primary sources are rare. And because of the ever-shifting language surrounding gayness, the documents that do exist in archival repositories are often difficult to locate because of ignorance or bias in the cataloging process. Finding aids to queer holdings are helpful, but such aids are few and far between.

Karin Wulf, a librarian and history professor at Brown University, writes: "'Archival silence' has become a shorthand for absences in archival records. It also refers to biases in collections, collecting habits, and institutions that occlude people and their histories, and the power dynamics that are as present in the materials and the institutions as they are in the economic, social, political, and other relationships and structures they document. Archives can and do, as Michel-Rolph Trouillot put it, silence the past."[3]

ORAL HISTORY

A recent trend in queer studies—both institutionally and among public researchers—is the use of oral histories. According to the Oral History Association: "Oral history is a field of study and a method of gathering, preserving and interpreting the voices and memories of people, communities, and participants in past events. Oral history is both the oldest type of historical inquiry, predating the written word, and one of the most modern, initiated with tape recorders in the 1940s and now using 21st-century digital technologies."[4]

In Louisiana, a number of oral history initiatives have been launched in recent years. Last Call: The Dyke Bar History Project was prompted by the closure of New Orleans last lesbian bar, Ruby Fruit Jungle, in 2012. In addition to a digital archive of full-length oral history interviews, Last Call also produced a podcast series to cull these interviews into curated stories and even produced live performances based on the stories it captured. Also in 2012, the LGBT+ Archives Project of Louisiana grew out of an oral history initiative called the Legacy Project. Today the LGBT+ Archives Project works with the T. Harry Williams Center for Oral History at Louisiana State University to collect and preserve oral histories. The Louisiana Trans Oral History Project was started in response to the wave of anti-trans legislation introduced in the early 2020s. The project conducted forty interviews across a five-parish area, the transcripts and audio files of which live permanently at the T. Harry Williams Center for Oral History. And in 2022, the Special Collections Division at the Edith Garland Dupré Library received a grant from the American Library Association to document the queer history of southwestern Louisiana. Called "Queering the Collection," the program includes collecting oral histories as well as archival materials.

While oral histories can certainly make up for some of the gaps in the written, archival record, they are not perfect. Eyewitness accounts and memories are notoriously unreliable. People can usually remember insignificant details like what they ate for lunch yesterday, but such memories fade quickly. A person might remember the restaurant she went to years ago for a special occasion, but other circumstances surrounding that occasion, like what she ordered, become fuzzy over time. Some memories persist "because of their relevance to our conception of ourselves, [but they] have been reviewed and pondered to the point that they have become indelible."[5] Our notions of self are constantly under construction, and our lived experiences, our memories, are the building blocks. Oral historian Valerie Yow observes: "And yet, is it not the meaning attributed to the facts that makes them significant or not? After all, history—or society—does not exist outside human consciousness. History is what the people who lived it make of it and what the others who observe the participants or listen to them or study their records make of it. And present society is what we make of it."[6]

R. Kennedy Kirby sums up the problems with oral history interviews by asking: How can the interviewer ask relevant, informed questions yet still provide an atmosphere that will not improperly influence the informant's responses? How can the interviewer's biases be minimized? To what extent does the research agenda affect these biases? How can the oral historian evaluate the responses of the interview subject, which can be tainted in a variety of ways? Are interview subjects representative of the general population? And how are these subjects selected? To what extent do changes in values and norms over long periods of time alter perceptions? And related to all of this is the larger issue of the objectivity or subjectivity of all historical data, indeed of all human knowledge.[7] These issues are further complicated in documenting in queer history, especially if the interviewer is straight. Nan Boyd and Horacio Ramirez claim interviewers who are not queer cannot earn the necessary trust for authentic answers and that they might miss or not grasp the nuances of gay culture.[8]

And queer historians must also be mindful of the power dynamics of memory and how established power structures (twentieth-century straight patriarchal society, for example) manipulate and exploit collective memory "to discourage dissident groups who seek to challenge the prevailing hegemony."[9]

So, what does all this mean for the historical narrative set forth in this book? The research we conducted involved primary, written sources such as arrest records, newspaper articles, and property records, but we have also relied upon oral history interviews. Much of the material generated by these interviews has been corroborated with written sources but not all of it. And even the material that is corroborated is subject to problematic and nebulous interpretation. Consider the following example.

Was there a gay riot against the police at a gay bar on Bourbon Street fourteen years before Stonewall? Lasse Lau and Flo Maak think the answer is maybe. While conducting research at the LGBT History Archive in San Francisco, Lau, editor of *Queer Geographies,* ran across an oral history recorded in 1999 that caught his attention. The interviewee was Paul Coates, a navy veteran, dancer, and founder of the Ballet Academy and Theatre in Shreveport, Louisiana. In the interview, Coates recalls his regular trips to New Orleans for Mardi Gras and references a "gay riot" at Dixie's on Mardi Gras weekend, 1955. Dixie's Bar of Music was a popular gay bar on the corner of Bourbon and St. Peter Streets from 1949 to 1964. And for Mardi Gras, it was ground zero for gay men.

In his interview, Coates states: "Someone shouted out, 'The police is trying to get in here' so we said 'Well fuck them!' And so we got the bar stools and just piled them up against the door and we barricaded, we locked the door first . . . So the police were trying to break down the door . . . they threw in tear gas . . . we all got our handkerchiefs and covered our faces and we found the goddamn tear gas and threw it right back out the window at them."

I (Perez) read the interview transcript with amazement and bewilderment. A gay riot against the police on Bourbon Street? Fourteen years before Stonewall? During Mardi Gras? I had never heard of a riot at Dixie's. I asked around, and no one else had heard of it either. I checked with other local queer historians and even old-timers who frequented Dixie's. Again, no one had ever heard about a riot at Dixie's. I then became skeptical and chalked it up to a fanciful imagination. I was wrong. Sort of.

I told Lau that unless there was more documentary evidence, no one would believe the story. Then Howard P. Smith, a friend and fellow writer (Smith and I cowrote *Southern Decadence in New Orleans*), found a newspaper article referencing a riot on the same night Coates mentioned, but it had the riot taking place at Pat O' Brien's, a half-block away from Dixie's, in the 700 Block of St. Peter Street. Pat O'Brien's had a sidebar at the time reserved for "bachelors," a code word for gay men. A block away, a responding police car, with siren blasting, got stuck in crowd congestion at the corner of Bourbon and Toulouse (site of another popular gay bar, Tony Bacino's). A pedestrian, Eugene Breese, twenty-one, of Texas, yelled, "Cut out all that goddamn noise!" and "Fuck you!" A crowd formed. Officer Fernandez got out of his patrol car and approached Breese, who punched him in the face and was subsequently arrested, including being charged with "reviling the police." According to the police report, tear gas had been deployed forty-five minutes earlier in the 300 block of Bourbon Street. It was, apparently, an exceptionally raucous Mardi Gras weekend.

The newspaper article, the police report, and the arrest records raise just as many questions as they answer. And what of Coates's account? If the gay patrons at Dixie's did indeed fight back against the police that night, regardless of the police motive for entering the bar, it would constitute a significant rebellion in the annals of queer history on a par with the Compton Cafeteria and Stonewall Inn riots. But is Coates's testimony reliable? Lau and Maak are determined to find out. They are currently making a documentary film about Dixie's Bar of Music and queer New Orleans in the 1950s.[10]

Coates's oral history is illustrative of the problems with oral history and raises another important issue for anyone doing memory work—how "memory inform[s] the construction and maintenance of identities" and how "these identities are drawn upon and articulated through place." Scholars have noted that "memory has a use in a range of political, cultural, and social contexts, for endless reasons and purposes: to remember, to forget, to silence, to bolster, to control, to keep, to disseminate."[11]

Identity is a puzzle, and memories, and the stories we extrapolate from them, form the pieces by which we create a picture of ourselves. "Memories are who we are," says Rick Huganir, director of the Johns Hopkins Department of Neuroscience.[12]

MEMORY AND CONNECTION

Many of the men we interviewed came to New Orleans to escape the doldrums of the small towns in which they grew up. Just as many others came never intending to stay but did. Falling in love with New Orleans is easy to do, and it is certainly not a gay phenomenon; thousands of straight people as well have succumbed to New Orleans's well-chronicled seductions. Nonetheless, there is a certain affinity between gay men and New Orleans. This sense of belonging goes beyond the quaintness and charm of a lingering European atmosphere for which New Orleans is known. The connection is deeper, more psychic and rooted in a metaphorically shared experience. Historically, the gay experience in America is remarkably similar to the city's experience—namely, one of difference, indifference, and difficulty.

Just as gay people in America have always been, and continue to be, considered "other"—which is to say, be defined by what they are not and devalued because of that difference—so, too, has New Orleans been considered other. Both New Orleans and the gay person challenge and complicate the easy black-and-white dualistic mentality that permeates so much of Western thought.

Within a few years after its meager founding as a French colony, Louisiana (which then meant primarily New Orleans) was essentially abandoned by the French Crown and eventually handed over to Spain because it had become an unwanted burden. The colony proved to be just as much of an unprofitable nuisance to Spain, and after forty years, Spain gladly disowned the colony and gave it back to France, which, in a matter of weeks, eagerly sold it to the United States. Both France and Spain considered New Orleans a colonial failure, which is to say, not what they expected nor what they hoped for. The city resisted Americanization, and the ensuing Creole-American conflict remains legendary. Except for the golden decades before the Civil War, when New Orleans was a mighty economic power, New Orleans has consistently been a disappointment to its parent nation. Yet throughout that disappointment—perhaps because of it, perhaps in spite of it—New Orleans has managed to forge its own way and carve out an identity for itself that remains truly unique. Marinating for almost three hundred years now, New Orleans has endured great adversity—constant floods and hurricanes, fires, diseases, governmental neglect, political corruption, wars—and in the process has created a genuine culture that is wholly its own.

Some astronomers no longer refer to the universe; instead, they speak of the multiverse. The idea is that our universe is just one among many parallel universes. These sky wizards predict that eventually, billions upon billions upon trillions of years from now, after all the stars die, after all the planets and moons fall out of their orbits, after the remaining black holes fade away, all that will remain from all that is will be the fragmented and decayed remnants of time in the form of tiny photon particles traveling chaotically, spasmodically, in a quantum realm—silent echoes of existence, in memoriam.

The existence of our familiarity, that is, for there is so much more than we have dreamed of in our philosophies. One of the most exciting theories in cosmology today is M-theory, which posits that each universe is merely a bubble floating in an infinite cosmological membrane. And when these bubbles collide, there is, in one magical moment, a big bang, just like the one that gave birth to our little bubble 13.7 billion years ago—creation by collision, if you will, and so wonderfully random. What's more fascinating is that each universe bubble may have its own set of physical laws, laws that may be entirely foreign and antithetical to the ones Sir Isaac Newton made so clear for us all.

New Orleans is a universe unto itself—a parallel existence born of a collision of cultures that continues to morph and expand and create and delight and surprise. It's a place where the established rules don't apply and contradictions are the norm rather than the exception. Consider the following phenomenon: once a year, on All Saints' Day, New Orleanians picnic in the city's many graveyards at the tombs of their dead relatives. The Ursuline Convent, the oldest Catholic convent in the United States, is just a few blocks away from the nation's oldest gay bar. Piety Street is just one block from Desire Street. The sun rises on the west bank of the Mississippi River. Funerals are celebrated with jazz parades, and the dead are buried aboveground. Drive-through daiquiri shops are ubiquitous, and it's legal to buy a fifth of whiskey at a gas station at 4:00 a.m. on a Sunday. The rich and the poor share neighborhoods and shop at the same corner groceries and drink at the same corner bars. Perfect strangers greet each other with affectionate phrases like "Hey babe" or "Where yat dawlin." And each spring, the city's elite conservative businessmen don satin tights and very fey masks and prance around the streets throwing beads to, and partying with, the plebian masses.

In New Orleans, you learn to expect the unexpected. Contrary juxtapositions—sociological, moral, political, economic, religious, sexual—are manifold; they abound everywhere. Trying to make sense of them is for those who don't "get it." Apollo and Dionysus peacefully coexist here. To ask why or how is to ask the wrong question. In New Orleans, binary oppositions not only converge; they mutate into an ever-changing rhizomatic wonderland, the only proper response to which is a shrug of the shoulders and a smile.

Unlike the majority of straight people who get it but are still initially puzzled by the contradictions that make New Orleans, gay men understand such contradictions instinctively and completely. The city's culture of carnal indulgence, its constant threat of destruction, its fervent judgment by the morally self-righteous, its status as different—these are all characteristics with which gay men can immediately identify. For what else does it mean to be a young man in our heterosexual society coming to grips with his homosexuality than to worship the flesh, to fear for his emotional and physical life, to suffer the slings and arrows of rejection and alienation, to be agonizingly aware that he is not like other boys?

But beyond all this, there is something else that undergirds the bond between gay people and New Orleans: her unconditional acceptance and the open arms with which she receives and embraces people. New Orleans is a Siren City that smiles on all who visit her. She takes you in her arms and willfully gives up her secrets as she whispers in your ear: "It's okay. I'm not perfect either. Look at my scars and wounds and wrinkles. Let's forget the past with all its pain and live in the now. Come dream with me."

It is precisely this warm invitation that has inspired writers and artists for centuries. Many of them have commented on this notion of city as muse. Take, for instance, William Faulkner, who, once in a letter to his mother, described how accepted he felt in New Orleans, accepted in a way he had not experienced in other places. This phenomenon baffles many people. Such people often remark how distinctive New Orleans is, how unlike any other American city it is. Not just the food and music but something deeper. What they sense but can't quite put their finger on is the fact that New Orleans has always resisted "cookie-cutter-ness."

After the Industrial Revolution effectively ended Thomas Jefferson's vision of America as an agrarian utopia, New Orleans could have evolved into the Queen City of the South (for a brief while, it was), but to do so would have meant buying into the economic gospel of the capitalist barons who have succeeded in transforming America into a corporate feudalistic state. But old-fashioned, stubborn New Orleans resisted the sales pitch and ceded that honor to Atlanta and Houston, preferring instead to grow slowly, more authentically. New Orleans is many things, but cutting edge is not one of them.

Even today, the familiar landmarks of corporate landscapes and urban fiefdoms that make every American town look just like every other town are noticeably absent in New Orleans. Indigenous restaurants outnumber fast-food and chain restaurants by astronomical numbers. Ditto for hotel chains. Not a single Fortune 500 Company is based here. Giant supermarkets have tried for years to make inroads in the city, mostly to no avail. And when Walmart announced plans to open a "Super Center," the local population went ballistic, successfully delaying the store's opening for years. Shopping malls in the traditional sense are, for the most part, nowhere to be found in the city limits.

Like those who are proudly out, New Orleans is a city that knows itself well and is secure and confident enough in itself to extend an open hand and a warm smile to any and all, but at the same time, it is fiercely protective of its culture and heritage, and that doesn't include fealty to corporate overlords. Like the flamboyant drag queen who fiercely resolves to be herself regardless of what others think, so it is with New Orleans. Given the live-and-let-live attitude that defines New Orleans, it is no wonder gay men are drawn to the city.

Also cementing the strong bond between gay men and New Orleans is a common insight into the nature of reality and fantasy. At its core, New Orleans is a fascinating study in desire—its pull, its promises, its lies, and its consequences. Just as desire permeates the notion of gayness—defines it, really, for good or ill—so is desire inextricably linked with the heart of New Orleans. This fixation with desire is what fuels Carnival and Mardi Gras, the music and culinary scenes, the city's epic obesity and its rampant alcoholism.

Tennessee Williams came as close as anyone to explaining this phenomenon. It's no mistake he set his most famous play on Elysian Fields. Elysian Fields Avenue is where Stanley and Stella live in *A Streetcar Named Desire.* Upon arriving in New Orleans, Blanche DuBois says, "They told me to catch a streetcar named Desire and then transfer to one called Cemeteries." Anyone wanting to discover the secret to understanding and appreciating New Orleans should begin by considering the metaphorical implications of that quotation. The easy conclusion is that desire leads to death, but the Big Easy is not that easy. No, the truth of the matter is that the folks here are keenly aware of their own mortality, and it's that grim awareness that feeds the urgency of desire. Who knows what dreams may come in that sleep of death, so we better live it up while we have the time. Many of the men we interviewed for this book, especially the ones who moved here as adults, returned over and over again to the time when they were lost in the closet, fumbling around in the dark, some spending years living double lives or going through the motions of being married for appearance's sake.

Elysium is a good way to describe New Orleans, for both are mythical places that defy easy description or definition. For Homer and Pindar, Elysium was the final resting place for the souls of the heroic and the virtuous, a designation that would be complicated by later writers. Dante's Limbo in *The Divine Comedy* strongly resembles classical Elysium, with one important difference—as the upper circle of hell, sadness prevails for the virtuous pagans who find themselves there; heaven is close yet unattainable. Renaissance poets envisioned the place as a paradise filled with joyful indulgences. In the fiction of Tolkien, Elysium is a mythical land of gods and elves and other fantastical creatures.

In all these literary depictions, Elysium is positioned on the margins of the afterworld, located off-center, on the edge. And so it is with New Orleans: on the edge of the continent, on the edge of imagination, on the edge between life and death. To be queer in America is certainly to identify with such marginalization.

For Tennessee Williams, New Orleans is Elysium. For the gay man as well as for New Orleans, objective reality is adapted to the ideal, not the other way around. In other words, reality is adapted to the way things ought to be. Here the boundary between fantasy and reality is both malleable and permeable.

In *Streetcar,* Blanche DuBois comes to New Orleans to escape the reality of her past and to begin her gradual descent into madness. But that's ironic because although New Orleans is a city filled with people living in what appears to be a fantasy world, their Blanche DuBoisian denial of reality is not so much an escape as it is an alternative reality—an Elysium where broken dreams are welcomed and redeemed and given new life. The ghosts of past failures and previous loss are present for sure, but they are harmless, their power to haunt usurped by a new reality. At one point in the play, Blanche sings "It's Only a Paper Moon," whose lyrics declare if both lovers believe their imagined reality, then it's no longer make-believe. New Orleans and her many lovers couldn't agree more.

Much of New Orleans lies just at or slightly below sea level and is ever sinking, yet the people here, gay and straight, live with their heads in the clouds—hovering aloofly between heaven and earth, blithely ignoring that murky boundary between reality and fantasy, the line between life and death obscured by desire, all the while solemnly aware of their own impending mortality.

ACKNOWLEDGMENTS

Writing a book is a solitary practice; bringing a book to publication is not. Because this book builds on previous work, we have double the people to thank. We remain grateful to the many people who contributed to our earlier work, including Gilbert Estrada, Otis Fennel, Ken Grand Pré, Dr. John Meyers, Lee Miller, Ann E. Smith Case, and Zetta Brown; also Robert Ticknor of The Historic New Orleans Collection and independent researchers Alice Blackwell and Anna Mathias, who assisted with new research for the current volume. We are also thankful for the scores of men who agreed to be interviewed. Just as many people, who preferred not to be formally interviewed, offered encouragement throughout the research and writing process. We are also grateful to untold thousands of gay men over the decades who, by living their lives openly and with dignity, nudged the closet door ever more open. Their names have slipped from memory, and their lives remain unsung. Their legacy does not.

NOTES

INTRODUCTION

1. Johnson, *New Orleans.*

2. Windham, *Tennessee Williams' Letters.*

1. QUEER NEW ORLEANS BEFORE THE BARS

1. Perez, "What's in a Name? Bulbancha and Mobilian Jargon."

2. Bossu, *Travels in the Interior of North America.*

3. Picq and Tikuna, "Indigenous Sexualities."

4. Sauvole, *Journal of Sauvole.*

5. Montigny, *Les Missions du seminaire de Québec* (1699), quoted in Ellis, *The Great Power of Small Nations.*

6. Charlevoix, *Histoire et description generale de la Nouvelle France.*

7. Ethridge and Shuck-Hall, *Mapping the Mississippian Shatter Zone.*

8. Milne, "Picking Up the Pieces."

9. Perez, "Tattooed Arm & the Natchez Massacre."

10. Montigny, *Memoires historiques sur la Louisiane,* quoted in Ellis, *The Great Power of Small Nations.*

11. Giraud, *History of French Louisiana,* vol. 2.

12. Vallette de Laudun, *Journal d'un voyage a la Louisiane,* quoted in Ellis, *The Great Power of Small Nations.*

13. Translations of the *Proceedings of the French Superior Council,* April 1725. Louisiana State Museum Archives, box 1; Sparks, *Religion in Mississippi.*

14. Fieseler, "LGBTQ+ Rights Movement in Louisiana."

15. In 1994, New Orleans attorney John Rawls unsuccessfully challenged the state's sodomy statute.

16. Ciravolo, *Legacy of John McDonogh.*

17. Johnson, "What Happened to Whitman in New Orleans."

18. Adams, "New Orleans, Walt Whitman and Leaves of Grass."

19. Martin, "Whitman, Walt."

20. Whitman, *Leaves of Grass* (2009).

21. Ibid.

22. Whitman, "I Saw in Louisiana a Live Oak," *Leaves of Grass* (2023).

23. LeMaster and Kummings, *Walt Whitman.*

24. Batson, "New Orleans."

25. Reizenstein and Rowan, "'Lesbian Love,'" 284–96.

26. Rowan, "Introduction," *The Mysteries of New Orleans.*

27. Ibid.

28. Meran is a popular resort in Northern Italy.

29. Reizenstein, *The Mysteries of New Orleans.*

30. Rowan, "Introduction."

31. S. H. Lutzen, *Deutsch Zeitung,* February 1, 1854.

32. Reizenstein, *Louisiana Staats-Zeitung,* January 13, 1854.

33. Reizenstein, *Louisiana Staats-Zeitung,* February 2, 1854.

34. Rowan, "Introduction."

35. Ibid.

36. Brothers, *Louis Armstrong's New Orleans.*

37. "Tony Jackson," Chicago LGBT Hall of Fame, July 1, 2023, https://chicagolgbthalloffame.org/jackson-tony.

38. Batson, "New Orleans."

39. Coyle and Van Dyke, "Sex, Smashing, and Storyville."

40. Presbytery of New Orleans, *Minutes,* Reverend Carl Schlegel, 111–22.

41. Katz, "Carl Schlegel." According to Katz, Schlegel returned to Germany in 1903 to participate in meetings of the Scientific-Humanitarian Committee, the world's first homosexual rights organization, founded by Magnus Hirschfeld in Berlin in 1897. There Schlegel consulted with other members about formally organizing other gay ministers in the United States. Schlegel was also arrested while there for violating paragraph 175 of the German Criminal Code, which outlawed homosexual acts.

42. The Society for Human Rights was the nation's first gay liberation organization, predating the Mattachine Society by twenty-six years.

43. Kaiser, *Gay Metropolis.*

44. Fair, "New Orleans."

45. The Tango Belt was bounded by Canal, N. Rampart, Dauphine, and St. Louis Streets.

46. Thomas, *Lyle Saxon.*

47. Saxon's other books are *Father Mississippi* (1927), *Fabulous New Orleans* (1928), *Old Louisiana* (1929), *Lafitte the Pirate* (1930), *Children of Strangers* (1937), and *The Friends of Joe Gilmore* (1948).

48. The first opera ever performed in North America, André Ernest Grétry's *Sylvain,* debuted in New Orleans in 1796 at the Théâtre St. Pierre. Throughout the nineteenth century, opera

flourished at a number of theaters in New Orleans, and the city was considered the "opera capital" of North America.

49. Saxon, *Fabulous New Orleans.*

50. McCollum, "Richard Koch."

51. Bonner, "Arts and Crafts Club."

52. For more information on this legendary bohemian space, see Warner, "Heathen Crowd at the Green Shutter."

53. Hemard, "William Ratcliffe Irby." Hemard notes that Irby's donation to the Archdiocese and Tulane University were anonymous and not revealed until after his death, probably because he was Jewish. That Irby was also gay may have also been a factor in wishing to remain anonymous, but Hemard makes no mention of Irby's sexuality.

54. Irvin, "Pontalba Buildings."

55. Reed, *Dixie Bohemia.*

56. Codrescu, *New Orleans.*

57. Quoted in Fellows, *Passion to Preserve.*

58. Griffin, *Who Set You Flowin'.*

59. Todd A. Price, "New Orleans Bars Celebrate the 75th Anniversary of Prohibition's Repeal," *New Orleans Times-Picayune,* December 5, 2008.

60. Ibid.

61. Magill, "Liquor Capital of America."

62. Liebling, *Earl of Louisiana.*

63. Friedman, *Art of the State.*

64. Cowan and McGuire, *Louisiana Governors.*

65. Mizell-Nelson, "Alejandro O'Reilly."

66. Ellis, *Madame Vieux Carré.*

2. CAFÉ LAFITTE BEFORE THE EXILE

1. Reed, "French Quarter Renaissance."

2. Ellis, *Madame Vieux Carré.*

3. Morrison, *Early American Architecture.*

4. The bar claims this distinction but has not provided any supporting evidence or documentation.

5. "937–941 Bourbon St.," Collins C. Diboll Vieux Carré Digital Survey, accessed October 24, 2024, https://www.hnoc.org/vcs/property_info.php?lot=18806.

6. Edith Elliott Long, "Lafitte's Blacksmith Shop Legend or Fact," *Vieux Carré Courier,* August 20, 1965.

7. Ibid.

8. Property records indicate that Jean Lafitte did own a lot nearby, at what is now 926 Bourbon Street.

9. Lafcadio Hearn, "Scenes of Cable's Romances."

10. King and Ficklen, *History of Louisiana.*

11. Arthur, *Old New Orleans.*

12. Thomas Griffin, "Lagniappe," *New Orleans Item,* February 13, 1956.

13. Steinbeck, "America and the Americans."

14. This quotation is from a 1989 interview between Grace Zabriskie and Joe Frank. https://www.joefrank.com.

15. Mary Collins's obituary, *New Orleans Times-Picayune,* December 9, 1967.

16. Thomas Griffin, "Lagniappe," *New Orleans Item,* April 17, 1951.

17. Thomas Griffin, "Lagniappe," *New Orleans Item,* June 5, 1952.

18. Thomas Griffin, "Lagniappe," *New Orleans Item,* April 29, 1954.

19. Conveyance records indicate that on June 23, 1958, Bertrous G. Joseph sold the property at 941 Bourbon to Lafitte's Blacksmith Shop, Inc.

20. Classified advertisement, *New Orleans Item,* September 21, 1945.

21. Mary Collins obituary, *New Orleans Times-Picayune,* December 9, 1967.

22. Mary Collins interviewed by Joe Frank. https://www.joefrank.com.

23. Dixie Fasnacht and her sister Irma would relocate the bar to 701 Bourbon Street in 1949. It remained open until 1964.

24. Saxon, *Friends of Joe Gilmore.*

25. Ibid.

26. Ibid.

27. Alan Citron, "Captain George Tchakiris," *New Orleans States-Item,* December 18, 1971.

28. Montagu, *Greyhound Diary.*

29. Thomas Griffin, "Lagniappe," *New Orleans Item,* August 1, 1949.

30. Kinney, *Bachelor in New Orleans.*

31. Brennan, "Secret Ingredient."

32. Danton Walker, "That Streetcar Again," *New Orleans Item,* June 16, 1948.

33. Thomas Griffin, "Lagniappe," *New Orleans Item,* April 11, 1956.

34. Kemp, "Enrique Alferez."

35. Capote, *Dogs Bark.*

36. Perez, "Gay Lens."

37. In 1921, Whitesell moved into an apartment and opened a studio at 726 St. Peter Street, behind what would later become Preservation Hall. In 1961, Allan and Susan Jaffe purchased the property in order to open the legendary jazz venue. They soon discovered they had inadvertently inherited a collection of Whitesell's negatives and equipment, which they eventually donated to Tulane University. Decades later, after Hurricane Katrina, their son, Ben, discovered that four thousand more of Whitesell's negatives had been languishing in a storage unit above the club. In 2008, Julie Rendleman, a graduate student at Southern Illinois University Carbondale whose friend was managing Preservation Hall, learned of the previously lost collection and undertook an extensive restoration project.

38. Perez, "Gay Lens."

39. Kennedy, *Dining in New Orleans.*

40. Tallant, *Mr. Preen's Salon.*

41. "Café Lafitte Sold at Auction for $42,500," *New Orleans Item,* February 5, 1953.

42. "After Dark," *New Orleans Times-Picayune,* June 17, 1992.

3. POST-EXILE AND THE CLOSET

1. Le Blond de la Tour Map, January 1, 1722, Collins C. Diboll Vieux Carré Digital Survey.

2. Gonichon Map, January 1, 1731, Collins C. Diboll Vieux Carré Digital Survey.

3. Notarial Act, October 2, 1829, Theodore Seghers, notary public, Civil District Court Notarial Archives for Orleans Parish.

4. Succession, Second District Court, CDC no. 32592.

5. Conveyance Office Book, 1883, vol. 116, 901.

6. Soard's New Orleans City Directory, vol. 24, found in *City and Business Directories: Louisiana, 1805–1929.*

7. New Orleans *Times-Picayune,* June 9, 1918.

8. *New Orleans Times-Picayune,* April 6, 1923; "Six Dry Raids Reported Thursday by Officers," *New Orleans Item,* November 8, 1923.

9. New Orleans *Times-Picayune,* May 10, 1925; *New Orleans Item,* August 12, 1928; *New Orleans Item,* September 12, 1928.

10. *New Orleans City Directory, 1952.* Williams Research Center, Historic New Orleans Collection, accessed on August 29, 2023.

11. Business filings with the Louisiana Secretary of State's office list the "Bourbon Inn Social Club" as a nonprofit corporation. Original filing date is November 15, 1946.

12. Caplinger obituary, *New Orleans Item,* March 27, 1956.

13. Perez and Palmquist, *In Exile: The History and Lore.*

14. Delery, *Out for Queer Blood.*

15. "Today's Chuckle," *New Orleans States-Item,* January 24, 1959.

16. Perez and Palmquist, *In Exile: The History and Lore.*

17. Doyle, *1981.*

18. White, *States of Desire.*

19. Albert Carey, interview with the authors, n.d.

20. Ibid.

21. John Meyers, interview with the authors, January 2011.

22. The drinking age in Louisiana was eighteen at this time.

23. Perez and Palmquist, *In Exile: The History and Lore.*

24. Fair, "New Orleans."

25. Perez and Palmquist, *In Exile: The History and Lore.*

26. "Dayries Cites No.1 Vice Problem," *New Orleans Times-Picayune,* June 30, 1955.

27. "Curb Advocated on Homosexuals: Crackdown to Save Young Persons Demanded," *New Orleans Times-Picayune,* April 28, 1951.

28. "Vieux Carré Unit Seeks Ordinance," *New Orleans Times-Picayune,* March 8, 1951.

29. Perez and Palmquist, *In Exile: The History and Lore.*

30. City ordinance, section 5-66, CCS 18, 537.

31. Perez and Palmquist, *In Exile: The History and Lore.*

32. Ibid.

33. Perez and Palmquist, *In Exile: The History and Lore.*

34. Ibid.

35. Perez, "Dixie's, Yuga, and Gay Carnival."

36. Carey, "New Orleans Mardi Gras Krewes."

37. Smith, *Unveiling the Muse.*

38. White, *States of Desire.*

39. Starr, *New Orleans Unmasqued.*

40. Caillot, *Company Man,* 134–36.

41. Perez and Palmquist, *In Exile: The History and Lore.*

42. Smith, "Golden Celebration."

43. For more information on Gay Carnival, see Smith, *Unveiling the Muse.*

44. Ibid.

45. Some versions of the story, notably the passage from Poppy Z. Brite's *Prime: A Novel,* have Garrison throwing a glass of wine in his wife's face.

46. Perez and Palmquist, *In Exile: The History and Lore.*

47. Lambert, *False Witness.*

48. Robert Batson, "Claiming Our Past," *Impact,* July–August 1994.

49. Perez and Palmquist, *In Exile: The History and Lore.*

50. Ibid.

51. Ibid.

52. Ed Anderson, "Additional Gay Youth Ring Charges Hinted," *New Orleans Times-Picayune,* November 3, 1977.

53. Bob Ussery, "Police Crackdown on Gays in Par Is Due to 'Calls,'" *New Orleans Times-Picayune,* August 17, 1976.

54. "Gay Liberation Group Marches," *New Orleans Times-Picayune,* January 24, 1971.

55. Fieseler, *Tinderbox.*

56. The Daughters of Bilitis was the first lesbian rights group in the United States.

57. Perez and Palmquist, *In Exile: The History and Lore.*

58. Ibid.

59. For more information on Bill Rushton's activism, see Perez, "Bill Rushton."

60. Sears, *Rebels, Rubyfruit, and Rhinestones.*

61. For more information about the Up Stairs Lounge fire, see LGBT+ Archives Project of Louisiana, accessed August 17, 2025, https://lgbtarchiveslouisiana.org/the-upstairs-lounge-fire.

62. Sears, *Rebels, Rubyfruit, and Rhinestones.*

63. For more information on the history of Southern Decadence, see Smith and Perez, *Southern Decadence.*

4. THE WOOD YEARS

1. Thomas Wood, interview with the authors, July 23, 2024.

2. Ibid.

3. Ibid.

4. Regina Adams, interview with the authors, January 18, 2025.

5. Ibid.

6. Ibid.

7. Ibid.

8. "Quarterites Ask Protection from Slasher," *New Orleans Times-Picayune,* April 10, 1977.

9. John Meyers, interview with the authors, September 2010.

10. Ibid.

11. Ibid.

12. Ken Marino, interview with the authors, November 12, 2024.

13. Lloyd Sensat, interview with the authors, November 2010.

14. Ibid.

15. Cizek and Sensat were instrumental in the "gayification" of the Marigny neighborhood. Both men had a passion for historic preservation and restored two homes in the district. Cizek is a retired professor of architecture from Tulane University, where he directed the Preservation Studies program. Sensat passed away in 2011 and is buried in the Marigny family tomb at St. Louis Cemetery No. 1.

16. Ibid.

17. Darrel Thaxton, interview with the authors, December 24, 2024.

18. "Photos: The Unexpected Beauty of George Dureau," *The Advocate,* July 5, 2016, Arthur Roger Gallery website, https://arthurrogergallery.com/2016/07/photos-unexpected-beauty-george-dureau-advocate.

19. Douglas MacCash, "Opening the Shutter," *New Orleans Times-Picayune,* October 22, 1999.

20. Perez and Palmquist, *In Exile: The History and Lore.*

21. Letter to the editor, *Louisiana Gay Blade,* 1977.

22. Fieseler, "Up Stairs Lounge Fire."

23. Tom Cucullu, interview with the authors, December 20, 2024.

24. Ibid.

25. Ibid.

26. Thomas Wood, text message to the authors, August 10, 2024.

27. This passage on the boycott was adapted from Perez, *Political Animal.*

28. Roberts Batson, interview with the authors, December 2024.

29. "Show of Shows," *New Orleans Times-Picayune,* February 20, 1977.

30. Ibid.

31. David Cuthbert, "Delirious Diversity: Bourbon Street Awards," *New Orleans Times-Picayune,* February 13, 1996.

32. Ken Marino, interview with the authors, November 12, 2024.

33. Thomas Wood, text message to the authors, July 23, 2024.

34. Two newspaper articles mention Morgan as a co-owner of the bar, but Wood says that was not the case. Several locals also mentioned Morgan as a co-owner of Café Lafitte in Exile, but this may have been an assumption based on the fact that Morgan and Wood lived together.

35. Ed Anderson, "Jury Awards Bar Operator $7,500 in Suit Against Cops," *New Orleans Times-Picayune,* July 20, 1982.

36. Letters from Roger Nelson to *Ambush Magazine,* August 22, 1998, and *Impact,* August 24, 1998, quoted in Perez, *Political Animal.*

37. Jack Sullivan, interview with the authors, April 2010.

38. Coleman Warner, "Proposed Roof on Bar Balcony Stirs Up Trouble," *New Orleans Times-Picayune,* September 14, 1995.

39. Coleman Warner, "Roof on Bar's Balcony Rejected," *New Orleans Times-Picayune,* September 20, 1995.

40. Louis, interview with the authors, April 2010.

41. Scotty, interview with the authors, March 2010.

42. Perez and Palmquist, *In Exile: The History and Lore.*

43. Robertson v. Wood ABC XYZ, Court of Appeal of Louisiana, Fourth Circuit, docket number 2000-CA-0995, October 24, 2001.

44. Louis interview.

45. William Fitch, interview with the authors, April 2010.

46. For a more detailed narrative history of how the AIDS crisis unfolded in New Orleans and how the city responded to it, see Perez, *Political Animal,* 135–47.

47. Will Bennett, interview with the authors, May 2010.

48. Albert Carey, interview with the authors, n.d.

49. Jody Gates, interview with the authors, April 8, 2020.

50. Marcy Marcel, interview with the authors, 2010.

51. Jack Sullivan, interview with the authors, September 2010.

52. Eric Hess, interview with the authors, September 2010.

53. Thomas Wood, text message to the authors, August 10, 2024.

54. Harry Hodges, interview with the authors, July 15, 2024.

55. Elizabeth Lanoix, interview with the authors, February 2011.

56. Shane Scallan, interview with the authors, 2012.

57. William J. Bryan v. Wood Enterprises, et al., United States District Court Eastern District, No. 08-3928, section "C" (5), September 27, 2010.

58. Marino interview.

59. Wood, interview.

5. THE SHIFTING ROLE OF THE GAY BAR

1. Javier Sandoval, interview with the authors, April 2010.

2. Heath, interview with the authors, 2010.

3. John Gotthelf, interview with the authors, 2010.

4. Hartless, "Questionably Queer," 1035–57.

5. The hearing was held in New Orleans on December 19, 2018.

6. Perez, "Rawhide and Phoenix."

7. Although the letterhead and signature have been redacted, ATC chair Lombard confirmed during the administrative hearing that Wood had filed the complaint.

8. Perez, "Rawhide and Phoenix."

9. Ibid.

10. Murphy, "Economic Impact of COVID-19," https://www.marketplace.org/2020/04/01/the-economic-impact-of-covid-19-is-magnified-in-new-orleans.

11. Lucas Harrell, "PRIDE Northshore Rolls in Mandeville for First Time," *Fight Back! News,* June 4, 2024, https://fightbacknews.org/articles/pride-northshore-rolls-in-mandeville-for-first-time.

12. Willem Myers, interview with the authors, June 18, 2024.

13. Michael Santone, interview with the authors, July 2010.

14. John Gotthelf, interview with the authors, 2010.

15. Myke Kolb, interview with the authors, 2010.

16. Tim Kinzel, interview with the authors, 2011.

17. Campbell, *Double Life.*

18. Hartless, "Questionably Queer," 1035–57. See also Hubbard, "Here, There, Everywhere," 640–58.

19. Ibid. See also Bettani, "Straight Subjectivities in Homonormative Spaces," 239–54; and Holt and Griffin, "Being Gay, Being Straight and Being Yourself," 404–25.

20. Visser, "Homonormalisation of White Heterosexual Leisure Spaces in Bloemfontein," 1347–61.

EPILOGUE

1. "Oral History Reliability Is Under Question," *Library Journal,* June 15, 1980.

2. Handlin, *Truth in History.*

3. Wulf, "Archival Shouting," https://www.historians.org/perspectives-article/archival-shouting-silence-and-volume-in-collections-and-institutions-april-2024.

4. Oral History Association, accessed March 27, 2025, https://oralhistory.org.

5. Hoffman and Hoffman, "Reliability and Validity on Oral History."

6. Yow, *Recording Oral History.*

7. Kirby, "Phenomenology and the Problems of Oral History."

8. Boyd and Ramirez, *Bodies of Evidence.*

9. Drozdzewski, De Nardi, and Waterton, "Geographies of Memory, Place and Identity."

10. Perez, "Forgotten Gay Riot."

11. Drozdzewski, De Nardi, and Waterton, "Geographies of Memory, Place and Identity."

12. "Inside the Science of Memory," Johns Hopkins Medicine, accessed March 22, 2015, https://www.hopkinsmedicine.org/health/wellness-and-prevention/inside-the-science-of-memory.

WORKS CITED

Adams, Nordette. "New Orleans, Walt Whitman and *Leaves of Grass.*" Examiner.com, April 11, 2009.

Arthur, Stanley Clisby. *Old New Orleans: A History of the Vieux Carré.* Harmanson, 1944.

Batson, Roberts. "New Orleans." glbtq Encyclopedia Project, July 1, 2023, http://www.glbtqarchive.com/ssh/new_orleans_S.pdf.

Bettani, Stefano. "Straight Subjectivities in Homonormative Spaces: Moving Towards a New, 'Dynamic' Heteronormativity?" *Gender, Place & Culture* 22, no. 2 (2015): 239–54.

Bonner, Judith H. "The Arts and Crafts Club." *64 Parishes,* January 3, 2011.

Bossu, Jean Bernard. *Travels in the Interior of North America, 1751–1762.* Translated by Seymour Feiler. University of Oklahoma Press, 1962.

Boyd, Nan Alamilla, and Horacio N. Roque Ramirez, eds. *Bodies of Evidence: The Practice of Queer Oral History.* Oxford University Press, 2012.

Brennan, Ella. "The Secret Ingredient." In *My New Orleans,* edited by Rosemary James. Touchstone, 2006.

Brothers, Thomas. *Louis Armstrong's New Orleans.* New York: Norton, 2006.

Butler, Judith. *Gender Trouble: Feminism and the Subversion of Identity.* Routledge, 1990.

Caillot, Marc-Antoine. *A Company Man: The Remarkable French-Atlantic Voyage of a Clerk for the Company of the Indies.* Edited by Erin M. Greenwald and translated by Teri F. Chalmers. Historic New Orleans Collection, 2013.

Campbell, David L. *The Double Life.* Self-published, 2016.

Capote, Truman. *The Dogs Bark.* Plume, 1977.

Carey, Albert. "New Orleans Mardi Gras Krewes." glbtq Encyclopedia Project, 2006.

Charlevoix, Pierre-François Xavier de. *Histoire et description generale de la Nouvelle France avec le Journal historique d'un voyage fait par ordre du Roi dans l'Amerique Septentrionnale.* Giffart, 1744.

Ciravolo, G. Leighton. *The Legacy of John McDonogh.* Center for Louisiana Studies at the University of Louisiana at Lafayette, Louisiana Life Series, no. 12, 2002.

Clendinen, Dudley, and Adam Nagourney. *Out for Good.* New York: Simon & Schuster, 1999.

Codrescu, Andrei. *New Orleans: Mon Amor.* Algonquin Books, 2006.

Cowan, Walter Grieves, and Jack McGuire. *Louisiana Governors: Rulers, Rascals, and Reformers.* University Press of Mississippi, 2008.

Coyle, Katie, and Nadiene Van Dyke. "Sex, Smashing, and Storyville in Turn-of-the-Century New Orleans: Reexamining the Continuum of Lesbian Sexuality." In *Carryin' On in the Lesbian and Gay South,* edited by John Howard. New York University Press, 1997.

Delery, Clayton. *Out for Queer Blood: The Murder of Fernando Rios and the Failure of New Orleans Justice.* Exposit, 2017.

Doyle, JD. *1981—My Gay American Road Trip: A Slice of Our Pre-AIDS Culture.* QMH Press, 2023.

Drozdzewski, Danielle, Sarah De Nardi, and Emma Waterton. "Geographies of Memory, Place and Identity, Intersections in Remembering War and Conflict." *Geography Compass* 10, no. 11 (2016): 447–56.

Ellis, Scott S. *Madame Vieux Carré: The French Quarter in the Twentieth Century.* University Press of Mississippi, 2010.

Ethridge, Robbie, and Sheri M. Shuck-Hall, eds. *Mapping the Mississippian Shatter Zone: The Colonial Indian Slave Trade and Regional Instability in the American South.* University of Nebraska Press, 2009.

Fair, Lucy J. "New Orleans." *Encyclopedia of Homosexuality.* Garland, 1990.

Fellows, Will. *A Passion to Preserve: Gay Men as Keepers of Culture.* University of Wisconsin Press, 2004.

Fieseler, Robert W. "LGBTQ+ Rights Movement in Louisiana." *64 Parishes,* April 9, 2021.

——. "The Up Stairs Lounge Fire Killed 32 People. Its Legacy Still Haunts Black Gay New Orleans." *Daily Beast,* May 11, 2019.

Friedman, Nany. *Art of the State: Louisiana.* Harry N. Abrams, 1998.

Giraud, Marcel. *History of French Louisiana.* Vol. 2: *Years of Transition: 1715–1717.* Translated by Brian Pierce. Louisiana State University Press, 1993.

Griffin, Farah Jasmine. *Who Set You Flowin'? The African-American Migration Narrative.* Oxford University Press, 1995.

Handlin, Oscar. *Truth in History.* Harvard University Press, 1979.

Hartless, Jaime. "Questionably Queer: Understanding Straight Presence in the Post-Gay Bar." *Journal of Homosexuality* 66, no. 8 (2019): 1035–57.

Hearn, Lafcadio. "The Scenes of Cable's Romances." *Century Magazine,* November 1, 1883.

Hemard, Ned. "William Ratcliffe Irby." *64 Parishes,* November 8, 2013.

Hoffman, Alice M., and Howard S. Hoffman. "Reliability and Validity on Oral History: The Case for Memory." *Archives of Memory: A Soldier Recalls World War II.* University Press of Kentucky, 1990.

Holt, Martin, and Christine Griffin. "Being Gay, Being Straight and Being Yourself: Local and Global Reflections on Identity, Authenticity and the Lesbian and Gay Scene." *European Journal of Cultural Studies* 6, no. 3 (2003): 404–25.

Howard, John, ed. *Carryin' On in the Lesbian and Gay South.* New York University Press, 1997.

Irvin, Hilary. "Pontalba Buildings." *64 Parishes,* February 2, 2011.

Johnson, T. R. "What Happened to Whitman in New Orleans?" *School of Liberal Arts Magazine* (Spring 2020).

———, ed. *New Orleans: A Literary History.* Cambridge University Press, 2019.

Kaiser, Charles. *The Gay Metropolis.* Houghton Mifflin, 1997.

Katz, Jonathan Ned. "Carl Schlegel: Pioneering U.S. Gay Activist, 1906–7." *OutHistory,* July 1, 2023. https://outhistory.org/exhibits/show/schlegel/schlegelchrono.

Kemp, John R. "Enrique Alferez." *64 Parishes,* September 12, 2012.

Kennedy, Scoop. *Dining in New Orleans.* Bormon House, 1938.

King, Grace, and John Ficklen. *History of Louisiana.* L. Graham & Sons, 1893.

Kinney, Robert. *The Bachelor in New Orleans.* Bob Riley Studios, 1942.

Kirby, R. Kenneth. "Phenomenology and the Problems of Oral History." *Oral History Review* 35, no. 1 (Winter–Spring 2009).

Lambert, Patricia. *False Witness: The Real Story of Jim Garrison's Investigation and Oliver Stone's Film JFK.* M. Evans and Co., 1998.

LeMaster, J. R., and Donald D. Kummings, eds. *Walt Whitman: An Encyclopedia.* Garland, 1998.

Liebling, A. J. *The Earl of Louisiana.* Louisiana State University Press, 1970.

Long, Edith Elliott. "Lafitte's Blacksmith Shop: Legend or Fact." *Vieux Carré Courier,* August 20, 1965.

Magill, John. "The Liquor Capital of America—New Orleans during Prohibition." *Historic New Orleans Collection Quarterly* (Summer 1988).

Martin, Robert K. "Whitman, Walt." 1995. glbtq Encyclopedia Project, 2002. https://web.archive.org/web/20071012220801/http://glbtq.com/literature/whitman_w.html.

McCollum, Julie H. "Richard Koch." *64 Parishes,* January 31, 2011.

Milne, George Edward. "Picking Up the Pieces: Natchez Coalescence in the Shatter Zone." In *Mapping the Mississippian Shatter Zone: The Colonial Indian Slave Trade and Regional Instability in the American South,* edited by Robbie Ethridge and Sheri M. Shuck-Hall. University of Nebraska Press, 2009.

Mizell-Nelson, Catherine. "Alejandro O'Reilly." *64 Parishes,* February 25, 2013.

Montagu, Judith. *The Greyhound Diary.* Edited by Anna Mathias. Zuleika, 2025.

Montigny, Jean-François-Benjamin Dumont de. "Les Missions du seminaire de Quebec." 1699. Quoted in Elizabeth N. Ellis's *The Great Power of Small Nations.* University of Pennsylvania Press, 2023.

Morrison, Hugh. Early *American Architecture: From the First Colonial Settlements to the National Period.* Dover, 1987.

Murphy, Rhodes. "The Economic Impact of COVID-19 Is Magnified in New Orleans." *Marketplace,* April 1, 2020. https://www.marketplace.org/2020/04/01/the-economic-impact-of-covid-19-is-magnified-in-new-orleans.

Perez, Frank. "Bill Rushton: Journalist and Activist." *French Quarter Journal,* August 2023.

———. "Dixie's, Yuga, and Gay Carnival." *French Quarter Journal,* January 26, 2020.

———. "The Gay Lens: Frances Benjamin Johnston and Joseph 'Pops' Whitesell." *Ambush Magazine,* April 2, 2013.

———. *Political Animal: The Life and Times of Stewart Butler.* University Press of Mississippi, 2022.

———. "Rawhide and Phoenix: An Investigation." *Ambush Magazine,* March 26, 2019.

———. "The Tattooed Arm & the Natchez Massacre." *French Quarter Journal,* July 2023.

———. "What's in a Name? Bulbancha and Mobilian Jargon." *French Quarter Journal,* March 2023.

Perez, Frank, and Jeffrey Palmquist. *In Exile: The History and Lore Surrounding New Orleans Gay Culture and Its Oldest Gay Bar.* LL Publications, 2012.

Picq, Manuela Lavinas, and Josi Tikuna. "Indigenous Sexualities: Resisting Conquest and Translation." In *Sexuality and Translation in World Politics,* edited by Caroline Cottet and Manuela Lavinas Picq. E-International Publishing, 2019.

Presbytery of New Orleans, *Minutes of the Presbytery of New Orleans Pro-Re-Nata Meeting,* January 7, 8, 24, 25, and 29, 1907. E. S. Upton, 1907.

Proceedings of the French Superior Council, April 1725.

Reed, John Shelton. *Dixie Bohemia: A French Quarter Circle in the 1920s.* Louisiana State University Press, 2012.

———. "French Quarter Renaissance." *64 Parishes,* June 4, 2013.

Reizenstein, Ludwig von, and Steven Rowan. "'Lesbian Love' from *The Mysteries of New Orleans." Antioch Review* 53, no. 3 (1995): 284–96. JSTOR, https://doi.org/10.2307/4613166.

Rowan, Steven. "Introduction." *The Mysteries of New Orleans.* Johns Hopkins University Press, 2002.

Saxon, Lyle. *Fabulous New Orleans.* Robert L. Crager and Co., 1950.

——. *The Friends of Joe Gilmore and Some Friends of Lyle Saxon.* Pelican Publishing, 1998.

Sears, James T. *Rebels, Rubyfruit, and Rhinestones: Queering Space in the Stonewall South.* Rutgers University Press, 2001.

Smith, Howard P. "Golden Celebration." *Arthur Hardy's Mardi Gras Guide,* 2011.

——. *Unveiling the Muse: The Lost History of Gay Carnival in New Orleans.* University of Mississippi Press, 2017.

Starr, S. Frederick. *New Orleans UnMasqued: Being a Wagwit's Sketches of a Singular American City.* Dedeaux, 1985.

Steinbeck, John. "America and the Americans." *Saturday Evening Post,* July 2, 1966.

Tallant, Robert. *Mr. Preen's Salon.* Doubleday, 1949.

Thomas, James W. *Lyle Saxon: A Critical Biography.* Summa Publications, 1991.

Vallette de Laudun. *Journal d'un voyage a la Louisiane, fait en 1720.* Musier, Fils, & Fournier, 1768. Quoted in Elizabeth N. Ellis's *The Great Power of Small Nations.* University of Pennsylvania Press, 2023.

Villantray, Sauvole de la. *The Journal of Sauvole: Historical Journal of the Establishment of the French in Louisiana.* Edited by Jay Higginbotham. Colonial Books, 1969.

Visser, Gustav. "The Homonormalisation of White Heterosexual Leisure Spaces in Bloemfontein, South Africa." *Geoforum* 39, no. 3 (2008): 1347–61.

White, Edmund. *States of Desire: Travels in Gay America.* E. P. Dutton, 1980.

Whitman, Walt. *Leaves of Grass.* 1855. American Renaissance, 2009.

——. *Leaves of Grass.* 1855. Peter Pauper Press, 2023.

Windham, Donald, ed. *Tennessee Williams' Letters to Donald Windham, 1940–1965.* Holt, 1977.

Wulf, Karin. "Archival Shouting: Silence and Volume in Collections and Institutions." *Perspectives on History,* April 10, 2024.

Yow, Valerie Raleigh. *Recording Oral History: A Guide for the Humanities and Social Sciences.* 2nd ed. Alta Mira Press, 2005.

INDEX

Page numbers in italics refer to figures.